FEATURES

SPRING 2022 • NUMBER 31

T0153643

 Plough

WEB EXCLUSIVES

Read these articles at *plough.com/web31*.

Plough

PLOUGH.COM

EDITOR: Peter Mommsen
SENIOR EDITORS: Maureen Swinger, Sam Hine, Susannah Black
EDITOR-AT-LARGE: Caitrin Keiper
MANAGING EDITORS: Maria Hine, Dori Moody
BOOKS AND CULTURE EDITOR: Joy Marie Clarkson
POETRY EDITOR: A. M. Juster
DESIGNERS: Rosalind Stevenson, Miriam Burleson
CREATIVE DIRECTOR: Clare Stober
COPY EDITORS: Wilma Mommsen, Priscilla Jensen
FACT CHECKER: Suzanne Quinta
MARKETING DIRECTOR: Trevor Wiser
UK EDITION: Ian Barth
CONTRIBUTING EDITORS: Leah Libresco Sargeant,
Brandon McGinley, Jake Meador
FOUNDING EDITOR: Eberhard Arnold (1883–1935)

Plough Quarterly No. 31: Why We Make Music
Published by Plough Publishing House, ISBN 978-1-63608-051-2
Copyright © 2022 by Plough Publishing House. All rights reserved.

EDITORIAL OFFICE

151 Bowne Drive
Walden, NY 12586
T: 845.572.3455
info@plough.com

SUBSCRIBER SERVICES

PO Box 8542
Big Sandy, TX 75755
T: 800.521.8011
subscriptions@plough.com

United Kingdom

Brightling Road
Robertsbridge
TN32 5DR
T: +44(0)1580.883.344

Australia

4188 Gwydir Highway
Elsmore, NSW
2360 Australia
T: +61(0)2.6723.2213

Plough Quarterly (ISSN 2372-2584) is published quarterly by
Plough Publishing House, PO Box 398, Walden, NY 12586.
Individual subscription $32 / £24 / €28 per year.
Subscribers outside the United Kingdom and European Union pay in US dollars.
Periodicals postage paid at Walden, NY 12586 and at additional mailing offices.
POSTMASTER: Send address changes to
Plough Quarterly, PO Box 8542, Big Sandy, TX 75755.

Front cover: Artwork by Betty Acquah. Used by permission.
Inside front cover: Artwork by Marta Zamarska. Used by permission.
Back cover: Photography by Adrian Borda. Used by permission.

Elizabeth Catlett lithographs on pages 32 and 34: National Museum of Women in the Arts, Washington, D.C.
Museum purchase: Funds provided in memory of Florence Davis by her family, friends, and the Women's
Committee of the National Museum of Women in the Arts; Photograph by Lee Stalsworth.

Saint Rafael Arnáiz reading on page 107: Reprinted with permission of Liturgical Press.

ABOUT THE COVER:

The paintings of Ghanaian artist
Betty Acquah capture the soul
and energy that are both cause
and effect of true music-making,
the kind of music that flows
from the heart and draws others
in. This artwork was created by
Acquah for this issue of *Plough*.

FORUM ≋
LETTERS FROM READERS

This Forum features responses to *Plough's* Winter 2022 issue, "Made Perfect." Send your contributions to *letters@plough.com*, with your name and town or city. Contributions may be edited for length and clarity, and may be published in any medium.

FACING OUR LIMITATIONS

On Peter Mommsen's "Made Perfect": Isaiah's imagery of the Messiah as the one from whom we hide our faces has been borne out repeatedly through the Covid-19 pandemic. We are a death-denying, death-defying culture forced to reckon with tremendous loss. Yet staring death in the face is the memento mori that teaches us to number our days aright (Ps. 90:12). Had we faced our limitations sooner, we would be better prepared to prioritize the collective safety nets we need. Similarly, if we had taken seriously the perspectives, experiences, and expertise of the disability community, we would be in a better place to address our isolation and the current need for medical support and interdependence.

In an eternal sense, Christ is the one from whom people hide their faces. More immediately, modern societies continue to hide their faces from the revelation offered by the disability community. Thanks to *Plough* for amplifying these accounts.

Keith Dow , Ottawa, Ontario

SUBJECTS, NOT OBJECTS

On Maureen Swinger's "The Teacher Who Never Spoke": Much of undergraduate academia left me feeling voiceless. I was timid about entering adulthood. My students with disabilities have helped me build an interior life beyond what I thought possible. My experience suggests that a person's disability can open up emotional byroads that neurotypical people cannot access by themselves.

Whether they have physical disabilities or lack the words to say how they are feeling, my students' desire to have a relationship with me is heart-transforming. I don't know how it was for the generations that came before us, but I do know that we millennials are starving for relationship.

Tim Getz
Florida, New York

On Maureen Swinger's "The Art of Disability": Being blind from birth, but spared the consequences of a doctor's advice to my parents to institutionalize me, I read this piece with particular interest. It's obvious you are a caring advocate supportive of the spiritual and other benefits of parenting children with disabilities, as well as understanding some of the many social and physical difficulties involved.

I have a longstanding concern with the able-bodied perspective on people with disabilities as objects of care in the first place, that they become defined not by their names or abilities, but by their weakest link. I am sad that such depictions remove their humanity, free will, and agency – the able-bodied become the subjects who speak out on what disabled objects have brought into their lives.

Elizabeth L. Sammons
Columbus, Ohio
author, The Lyra and the Cross

WHY ME?

On Ross Douthat's "Hide and Seek with Providence": It takes a huge change of heart to move from primarily valuing people for their potential productivity, to valuing each person for their ability to love and be loved. Those of us with chronic illness find ourselves at the center of this existential question.

I have come to learn that I pay a high price for productivity and having fun. A few hours on a good day can leave me unable to focus and move for many days. My younger self could hide it much of the time, but for much of my life an autoimmune disorder has permitted my immune system to attack my body.

In this time of Covid, we hear often of cytokine storms. That's the description of an exaggerated immune response in which the body believes it is fighting an illness but which ultimately damages the whole. I'm writing this to promote understanding for the millions of people whose bodies, on a daily basis, create and fight these storms.

My disease believes that my joints are alien invaders. The attack is relentless. My body is at constant war with itself.

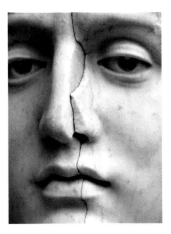

Those of us with autoimmune disorders don't necessarily look sick. In the age of Covid I hope everyone learns that there are many of us who always live in the middle of a storm, hoping for it to be tamed.

Emily Morrison
Arlington, Massachusetts

Douthat wants to know the reason he is afflicted with Lyme disease. . . . Our faith has long affirmed that God is a mystery, his purposes often inscrutable. We hold that in tension with our belief that God desires to be personally present to us – drawing near whenever and however he chooses. If our faith is to help us bear our suffering, the spiritual challenge isn't so much to seek out God's purpose as to trust in God's presence as best we can, and to redirect our energies from "why" to "how": How do we carry our burden in a way that honors God?

Michael Pennanen
Hammond, Indiana

IN BEAUTY GLORIFIED

On Isaac T. Soon's "The World Turned Right-Side Up": At the end of his essay, Soon notes that even in Christ's own glorified body, his wounds remain – no longer a source of suffering but a sign of victory. This ought to be the starting point for theological reflection upon the significance of both physical and cognitive handicaps. Historically it has been; Nancy Eiesland's *The Disabled God* (1994) inaugurated a tradition of seeing the glorified wounds of Christ as evidence of his solidarity with the disabled. Centuries before, both Aquinas and Augustine claimed that Christ's glorified wounds implied the martyrs would be risen with their own, for, he argued, "we shall see on the bodies of the martyrs the traces of the wounds which they bore for Christ's name, because they will not be a deformity, but a dignity in them; and a certain kind of beauty will shine in them."

But martyrs are not the only saints who bear in their bodies the marks of long faithfulness to Christ under duress and oppression. Some suffer far more from forms of societal exclusion and stigma than from anything within their bodies. Theological reflection upon Christ's "rich wounds yet visible above, in beauty glorified" permits Christians to see dignity rather than deformity in those with both physical and cognitive impairments. It is by now common for disability advocates, activists, and theorists to insist that disabilities ought not be understood as objects for cure. After all, what would it mean to "cure" a person's Down syndrome without thereby annihilating the person and personality who bears that Down syndrome? Instead, Christian theology insists that their bodies, along with the bodies of the typically abled, await glorification.

But there is yet one further implication of Soon's insight. If Christ resurrected is wounded and scarred, we have good reason to think everyone will likewise undergo a transformation. . . . Paul insists that we shall all be changed. God requires no more miracles to resurrect and glorify the body of a person with Down syndrome than are necessary to resurrect and glorify any non-disabled person. Conformity to Christ means conformity to his scars.

Justin R. Hawkins
New Haven, Connecticut

MUTUALITY AND COMMITMENT

On Issue 30: Made Perfect: For twenty years, I attended a church where a third of the attendees had various severe challenges. As long as we considered them part of our outreach, we were limited by our condescension from receiving the gifts they offered us. When we began to see them as God-given mentors, they began to realign our priorities: Will you love me? May I love you? Folks dealing with autism, Down syndrome, multiple sclerosis, muscular dystrophy, ALS, and more began leading congregational prayer, joining worship teams, serving communion, reading scripture, performing child dedications, anointing the sick, and commissioning other ministers.

Indeed, if Christ is truly reaching out to us, these were his agents, and we were all the richer for it.

Bradley Jersak
Abbotsford, British Columbia

My brother and sister were PKU babies who developed severe developmental and cognitive disabilities. Medical authorities told our parents, "Put them away. They won't live long." Instead, as their own calling to ministry, our parents kept Rosie and John in our home and later opened our home for the next fifty years to nearly twenty similar children. They were in the vanguard of parents who took up this calling and began supporting each other's families. My sister Rosie died this past October at age eighty. Having just reached age seventy-five my brother John is already energetically pursuing age seventy-six. Birthdays are important for him! Two pieces of advice: Together with the disabled member of your family, memorize and repeat often Jesus' words: "Suffer the little children to come unto me; and forbid them not. For of such is the Kingdom of God." You will find that the kingdom is already present in the supportive persons you meet along the way. And begin now to plan for the future, establishing an irrevocable trust that will support your family member into and during adulthood when you may no longer be there.

James Arthur Sterling
Mesa, Arizona

In 1985, my husband and I discovered an Ohio state program that removed people with developmental disabilities from institutions and placed them in homes. We investigated and after jumping through many hoops, met Terry. We got on well. He really liked our two-month-old son, Ruben.

Terry had Down syndrome. We didn't know a lot about it. We just brought him home and made him part of our family and community. He lived with us for seventeen years. We had two more babies, but Ruben was always his favorite. We liked to cross-country ski, so we got him skis and he joined the Special Olympics cross-country team. We liked to travel and camp so Terry got to experience many new places.

Not to paint our lives as perfect: Terry had celiac disease; his speech problems made him hard to understand at times. But it was an incredibly rewarding time. We saw Terry blossom in his skills and abilities. He had a community of people who knew and loved him.

As a result of our time with Terry, two other people in our community opened their homes to people with Down syndrome. And Ruben grew up to get a BA in theater from Kent State. He now teaches acting to adults on the autistic spectrum.

Elizabeth A. Ryan, Stow, Ohio

BEYOND A LABEL

On John Swinton's "A More Christian Approach to Mental Health Challenges": What a beautiful, rich, and insightful article. I have gone through life with a crazy aunt, a grandmother who is not all there, and a brother who is bipolar. These are the labels that others use to talk about them. As I watch them age and spend time with them, I see that we can still enjoy the beauties of life together. Watching the hummingbirds. Cuddling cats. Doing crossword or jigsaw puzzles. I have been convicted of a widely sweeping judgmentalism of their characters, intellect, even worthiness based on their mental health diagnoses. Swinton's writing strikes me with its compassion, humility, and genuine respect for individuals, no matter their issues. Keep writing, keep speaking.

Amanda McKinley
Austin, Texas

I joined the disability club last year when I lost my eyesight, so this issue couldn't have come at a better time for me. It's been both illuminating and challenging.

Several of your essays boldly pushed back against the prevailing idea that one must be productive – by which we usually mean something like contributing to the GDP – or one is somehow lesser. While I agree that our penchant for defining ourselves by our market value is terrible, I want to push back a little.

God created humankind out of nothing, set them up in a paradise, then said, "Get to work." Rather than rejecting the productivity idea altogether, I think we need to rethink what it means, so that everyone's acts count as contributions, from Peter's friend Duane to the woman (that's me) who has to have Siri do all her reading for her. What does that look like? I don't know. But I do know that it's infuriating to be told, "Don't feel like you need to contribute."

Brittany Petruzzi
Kernersville, North Carolina ➤

FAMILY & FRIENDS

AROUND THE WORLD

Iona, Scotland

Celtic Christianity on Iona

Iona Abbey served as a hub of wide-ranging activity in ancient times. Today it does again.

Kenneth Steven

I had experienced Iona as a remote place, out off the Scottish west coast and difficult to reach – the end of a long day's pilgrimage. I exulted in the quiet and rejoiced in the fact that this was the way things must have been from the beginning, when Saint Columba landed on the south coast of Iona in AD 563. It felt to me an edge place: when I stood on the west side of the island on a wild day looking out to sea, it might have been that there was nothing between me and America. All this suited the romantic notions I had about this island. This was for me both where I felt the deepest awareness of the divine and the place where words flowed from the pen.

Then one day I happened to be listening to a lecture by an archaeologist from the University of Glasgow. His first slide showed Iona, but not as I had seen it before on any map or as ever I had imagined it. Now Iona – an island a little over three miles long and perhaps one and a half miles in breadth – was at the very center of the map rather than the edge. To the south was the north coast of Ireland and the islands that lay between it and Iona; to the east was the jagged edge of the Scottish west coast.

The archaeologist explained how Iona had been at the very heart of the sea roads of the time. We are so ruled in our thinking, understandably enough, by paved roads. We live truly urbocentric lives: we go out to edge places and think of them as such. But early peoples thought in terms of the sea roads, and Iona was perfectly placed at the heart of them. And they were busy: the vessels that plied them were fetching and carrying, bearing travelers. Iona had been no edge place back then.

The Iona Community that grew out of the rebuilding of Iona Abbey in the 1930s, under the leadership of the extraordinary George MacLeod, sought to embody something of the core of Celtic Christian thinking. Of huge importance was the leaving behind of Iona to go back out

Kenneth Steven is a poet, novelist, and children's author from Scotland. His latest book is Iona: Poems. *He and his wife Kristina lead Celtic Christian retreats at the Argyll Hotel on Iona each October.*

Ruins still stand at the Iona nunnery and abbey.

into a troubled world: to Soweto, to São Paulo, to San Francisco. Iona was the well to which one came back to drink, but it was not the place where one rested forever. There was work to be done and urgency for the completion of that work.

In the same way Columba's monks had gone out or been sent out, not only to rocky islets to encounter a greater sense of God and his voice, but with the gospel, to convert. Doubtless it was to be there for others in every way, as Christ had been there for friend and stranger. For that reason the Iona Community was not resident on Iona: it was out in the world – challenging, questioning, building, and praying. And in the same way neither of these manifestations of Celtic Christianity is to be romanticized. Those early Celts were never gentle monks huddled in the granite headlands of Dalriada singing beautiful chants, any more

than George MacLeod's community who came after him. Iona Community members today are to be found protesting at the gates of weapons factories: for them Christianity is about love in action, overturning the tables in the temple.

The Catherine Project

Drawing on Aristotle, Dante, and Kierkegaard, the Catherine Project has created an online lyceum, and anyone who loves learning can join.

Zena Hitz

The pinnacle of intellectual life, so far as I am concerned, is to sit around a table talking about the deep questions, inspired by an excellent book. We are drawn to that table from a desire to understand and to learn, with and from one another. We read, speak, and listen, not to draw a boundary between ourselves and others, but to uncover bonds of human unity.

I had the privilege to attend St. John's College, a small liberal arts college with a similar vision of learning, and I teach there now. But I dreamt for years of ways to bring to the table anyone who wanted to join in the conversation. I envisioned education without strings attached, no grades, no credits, no tuition, run on the manifest love of learning alone. It took the summer of 2020 to see a way to

Zena Hitz is a tutor at St. John's College and the author of Lost in Thought: The Hidden Pleasures of an Intellectual Life *(2020). She also spent three years living and working in the Madonna House Apostolate and has taught in prison programs and other non-traditional settings.*

begin. I began organizing small online tutorials and reading groups via video conference. I found readers from various backgrounds on Twitter. We began with four tutorials on Homer and two reading groups, one on Aristophanes and one on Kafka. Since then we have hosted groups on Tolstoy, George Eliot, Rilke, Rousseau, Augustine, and Euclid, among others.

Late in the fall of 2020 the Kafka group wanted to move on to Kierkegaard, but sought more readers for the difficult endeavor. I posted on Twitter: "Who wants to read *Either/Or* on Saturday evenings?" I received more than a hundred messages. We called it "the Kierkegaard explosion," and organized several more groups to accommodate everyone. One evening last fall we held seminars on Genesis 1–5. We filled as many groups as we had leaders for, stopping at seventy readers. The appetite for learning is much larger than the capacities of our little organization.

Great books respond to one another and so form traditions, conversations among the wise over centuries. In the form of helpless books, they cannot refuse us entry. What we've called the Catherine Project seeks to introduce readers to the great traditions, European, Near Eastern, African, and Asian, each overlapping with one another. We are too small to take this on systematically, so we harness the enthusiasm of our volunteers, and make our way on small tracks, like a snowplow in a great mountain range.

We aspire to the simplicity of the great Christian martyr Catherine of Alexandria,

who is reported to have refuted fifty court philosophers with her eloquence. Her modern-day namesake, Catherine Doherty, followed a similar simplicity when she founded and ran a national lending library on donated resources at a time when public institutions left many regions of Canada neglected. Readers wrote to her from the remotest places; she found the books and mailed them out, one by one.

We work online, through video conference, as that way we reach people and places where intellectual community is hard to find. We hope in this way to form a network, and to discover areas where zealous readers might be concentrated. One day we hope to have physical homes, brick-and-mortar readers' libraries, where anyone can come to study and to meet others in study. In the meantime, we hope to host three-dimensional gatherings when and where it becomes feasible.

In the world of institutional higher education, humanistic learning is ever more difficult to find. Perhaps it will help institutions to change their tune if movements like ours grow large enough. If they do not, we help to shape communities that do not depend

on the university system alone for their intellectual engagement. Our studies benefit anyone, whatever their career path or lack thereof. Universities are wonderful, but they are not necessary in themselves for human flourishing.

Since our founding last year we have served 250 readers, many of whom study in multiple groups and return term after term. All of our group leaders and tutors are volunteers. We are committed never to charge tuition, although we welcome donations from readers in accordance with their means. We welcome new readers from all walks of life.

catherineproject.org

Poet in This Issue
Jacqueline Saphra

Saphra is a poet and playwright. Recent collections are *All My Mad Mothers*, shortlisted for the 2017 T. S. Eliot prize, and *Dad, Remember You Are Dead* (2019), both from Nine Arches Press. *A Bargain with the Light: Poems after Lee Miller* (2017) and *Veritas: Poems after Artemisia* (2020) are both published by Hercules Editions. Her most recent play, *The Noises,* was nominated for a Standing Ovation Award in 2021. Saphra's latest collection, *One Hundred Lockdown Sonnets,* was published by Nine Arches Press in 2021. She mentors and teaches for The Poetry School.

Her poem "Sunrise and Swag" appears on page 15, and "Poland, 1985" appears on page 41. ✐

Paolo Veronese, *Saint Catherine of Alexandria in Prison*, ca. 1580–85

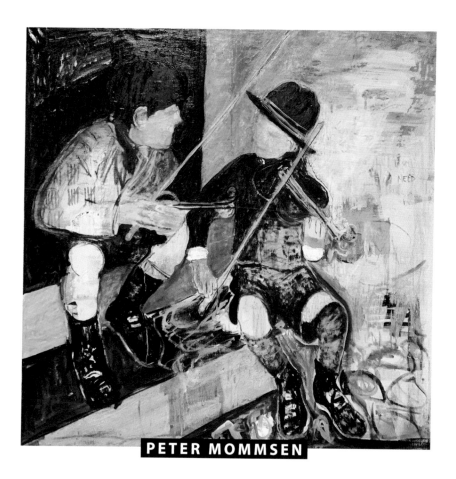

PETER MOMMSEN

Why We Make Music

A song has the power to shape the soul.

Borg de Nobel,
*Budapest Street
Fiddle Boys*,
ink on canvas,
2018

O N A JANUARY NIGHT in 1536 in Vienna, the schoolteacher Jeronimus Käls and two friends were arrested in a pub after refusing to join in a drinking game. Their refusal had raised the suspicion that they were Anabaptists, part of the radical wing of the Reformation; by imperial mandate, Anabaptism was a capital crime. "Praise be to God, we are indeed the right men!" Jeronimus told the officers who arrived two hours later to take them away.

Jeronimus and his friends spent the next three months in prison, where a team of judges and clergy interrogated them about their beliefs, including nonviolence and community of goods. A sympathetic judge appealed to Jeronimus to recant, urging him to remember his wife and children. When that effort failed, the three men were subjected to repeated torture and kept in separate cells to prevent them from speaking with each other. But they found a way to evade their jailers' restrictions: they sang.

"I rejoice with all my heart to hear you sing in the Lord, especially you, my dear brother Michael, when you sing evening songs," Jeronimus wrote to his fellow prisoners, in a letter he somehow persuaded a guard to pass to them. "I can understand almost every word if you are sitting right by the window and I listen carefully. . . . I love hearing each one of you, for I rejoice when I hear the Jerusalem song being sung, dear brothers. The very fact that it hurts Satan so much is a sure sign that it is pleasing to God; for they think they have prevented us from talking and comforting one another. So let us shout until we are hoarse!"

When he wasn't singing, Jeronimus composed songs himself. He managed to send one of his songs back home to his wife, Traindel, to share with their children. It was a nine-stanza acrostic of his name *Jeronimus,* declaring his joy at the privilege of suffering alongside Christ.

Songs like these formed the social media network of the Radical Reformation, whose underground leaders wrote relatively little in the way of systematic theology. What held the movement together, despite arrests, informants, and thousands of executions, was their culture of singing: hymns, versified Bible stories, and ballads of the heroes of the faith.

Such Anabaptist songs were just one stream in a massive musical outpouring in sixteenth-century Europe. Martin Luther pioneered singing as an instrument of social and religious change, using chorales and hymns for the common man and woman to accompany and propel his Reformation. Soon Catholic, Anglican, and radical reformers were offering their own musical innovations and revivals. As millions turned to faith with new fervor, they created a participatory culture of music-making that, though it evolved and secularized, has endured in various forms for five centuries.

In many places today, the culture of singing inherited from the Reformation remains robust, despite pressure from the commercial music industry. In the United States, group singing remains the most popular arts activity, and the number of people of varied ages and backgrounds who participate in community choirs is growing. While it's true that the number of church choirs has dipped as more congregations embrace band-driven worship music, the more remarkable fact is that almost half of the nation's 380,000 churches do boast a choir.

Or they did until the Covid pandemic hit. In spring 2020, church and community choirs shut down, concert halls went dark, and congregational singing became potentially dangerous to oneself or one's neighbor. It was as if all the pre-pandemic nightmares of music educators, churchgoers, cantors, and performing artists had suddenly come true. Under lockdown, we glimpsed what a world without communal music-making was like.

To underscore the loss, research showing the benefits of communal music has been steadily piling up. One study, for example, shows the power of group singing in building social relationships – no small thing when almost half of Americans say they are lonely. Another documents how group singing helps children develop their brains, emotions, and lungs. For adults, it is apparently as effective as light exercise in providing a sense of well-being, plus it's therapeutic for those with dementia and Parkinson's. As a 2020 *Nature* article summarizes:

> A growing body of evidence points to a wide range of benefits arising from participation in group singing. . . . Group singing might be taken – both literally and figuratively – as a potent form of "healthy public," creating an "ideal" community, which participants can subsequently mobilize as a positive resource for everyday life.

Well, yes, as Plato knew long before the social scientists arrived. As he wrote in the *Republic*:

"Training in music is most important, because rhythm and harmony permeate the innermost element of the soul, and affect it more powerfully than anything else." Music has a power of direct access to our emotional life; it gives us the ability to communicate with others in a way that goes beyond what we can conceptualize or verbalize. This is why, according to Plato, virtuous music is vital for building a virtuous community.

This intuition is widely shared across cultures. The Confucian "Record of Music," a text included in the *Li Ji* (*Book of Rites*) that may be contemporary with Plato, similarly links well-ordered music to a well-ordered society:

> Let music attain its full results, and there would be no discontent. . . . Violent oppression of the people would not arise; the princes would appear submissively at court as guests; there would be no occasion for the weapons of war, and no employment of the five punishments; the common people would have no distresses, and the son of Heaven no need to be angry – such a state of things would be a universal music.

Jewish and Christian traditions take the same insight even further: communal music serves to shape and build up the people of God. The Hebrew scriptures call dozens of times on the congregation of Israel to "sing to the Lord," with the Psalms playing a central role in Jewish liturgy to this day. The New Testament letters to the early churches repeat the same command: "With gratitude in your hearts sing psalms, hymns, and spiritual songs to God" (Col. 3:16).

To the early Christian writers, singing – along with the act of gathering, the breaking of bread, the common prayer, the laying on of hands, and the fraternal greeting – is a physical action that helps establish the fellowship of believers. In singing together, individuals who may be neither kin nor kind are welded together as one body.

THIS INSIGHT TURNS OUT to be true quite practically. I grew up, and still live, in a culture where communal singing feels natural. One of the side effects of being raised in a Bruderhof community is that by one's twenties, one can sing a couple of thousand songs by heart – folk songs, spirituals, hymns, carols, oldies, protest songs, and chunks of the big oratorios by Handel, Bach, or Mendelssohn. This memorization occurs whether one likes the songs or not, through repetition. As an Anabaptist church, we don't have a lectionary, prayer book, or much of a liturgy. But when we meet, which we generally do daily, we sing.

Yet singing isn't just a filler for awkward silences when no one has anything worthwhile to say (useful as that sometimes is). Far from being accidental, it is a communal habit that was cultivated by preceding generations, for reasons Plato would likely recognize. Consider the songbook I have from my grandmother, copied out on cheap paper in the 1940s, when she and her community were pioneering in Paraguay as refugees from the Third Reich. Hand-bound and rain-damaged, the book contains songs for every occasion: for the seasons and for stormy and sunny weather, work songs, fun songs, birthday songs, songs about Jesus, songs about Mary, prayers, lullabies, and songs to sing when someone dies, as two of her nine babies did.

She, like many Bruderhof women of her generation, wrote out her copy of the community song collection during moments snatched from chores during her weeks of maternity leave. At times, the ink color changes partway down a page, perhaps when she was interrupted by a baby's cries.

These are the songs she sang to her children, my mother sang to us, and we sang to (and still sing with) our kids. The books my grandmother and other mothers of those early years created are evidence that the gift of communal singing didn't come automatically. They're the basis of the printed songbooks the community still uses today.

ONE OF THE SONGS inherited from my grandmother's generation is a light-hearted setting of a rhyming German proverb: "Where people sing, you can happily relax – evil people have no songs." It has a catchy tune, and the proverb *sounds* true: if people are making music, that's got to be good. But the proverb is false, as people who had fled their homeland to escape song-singing Nazis surely knew.

Plato knew it too. The fact that music is so powerful in shaping our souls, he believed, is precisely what makes bad music so dangerous. Bad music feeds vices such as sloth, drunkenness, degeneracy, or cowardice. Plato linked it with particular rhythms and harmonies, which he proposed banning. In fact, the only music he wanted to allow would promote either martial courage or temperance and proper worship.

Luther, the great musician of the Reformation, agreed with Plato, at least on the general principle. One of his motives for composing his glorious hymns was to supplant the "bad music" of his day – secular folk songs and the courtly romances of the *Meistersinger,* which he thought fed sensuality. To that end, his "*cantica nova*" frequently stole the popular melodies of the "old songs" he sought to drive into extinction.

It's fun, and a little too easy, to mock would-be censors of bad music. After all, condemning whole genres usually proves to be folly. We can't judge the vanished Mixolydian melodies that Plato wanted to ban, but we can still listen to the Renaissance love songs that Luther frowned on. They are lovely – some are in my grandmother's songbook. More recent moral campaigns against pop or punk or rap may look no better with hindsight.

And yet Plato and Luther weren't entirely wrong. There is music that is bad for us. If music can shape our souls and our communities, then it matters where we bestow this power.

So how can we choose good music and avoid the bad? This is a thorny topic, but let's recklessly sketch out three practical rules. First, some music is bad for obvious reasons – it is, for example, debasing or narcissistic or death-obsessed. Here Plato's insight holds: people should not feed their minds with "symbols of evil, as it were in a pasturage of poisonous herbs, lest, grazing freely and cropping from many such day by day, they little by little and all unawares accumulate and build up a huge mass of evil in their own souls." We must beware becoming what we eat.

Then there's a badness that can lurk in Christian music. It comes from mistaking our aesthetic feelings for an experience of the holy – thinking one is experiencing God when in fact one is experiencing oneself. Obviously church music has always sought to dispose the emotions to prayer. But religious expressions should not be used lightly, especially in worship. The most sacred song can become spiritually dangerous if sung for artificial effect, as a replacement for the presence of the Spirit who originally inspired it. That's why religious music isn't necessarily better for us than profane music, and may at times be worse.

The songbook copied out by the author's grandmother, Annemarie Arnold (1940s)

A third hazard is uniquely modern, and stems not from the music itself but rather from how we interact with it. It's a result of the sheer ubiquity of music now available for consumption – its presence as a near-constant soundtrack to our daily lives, thanks to AirPods and Bluetooth and Spotify.

"Every age," C. S. Lewis writes, "is specially good at seeing certain truths and specially liable to make certain mistakes." In his time, Plato feared music's ability to produce excessive or decadent emotions. Our age may be prone to the opposite: the vice of apathy. To borrow the words of Roger Scruton, we *hear* the music but we don't *listen* to it. Digital music on tap is a temptation to chronic distraction of the soul, to a spiritual habit of superficiality and non-attention.

Fortunately, the remedy to this last danger is straightforward, though it takes effort: spend less time consuming prepackaged tunes and more time making music. This will be doubly rewarding if music-making is a communal enterprise – singing with one's family, singing in church, playing in a string quartet, starting a regular jam session. Personal media players tend to cut us off from the physical presence of others. But sharing in good music together breaks the spell of isolation and disembodiment. It builds friendship and community. It may create a legacy that outlasts us.

WHEN JERONIMUS KÄLS sent his wife his acrostic song from prison, he accompanied it with a farewell letter. "My own dear wife, my most beloved Traindel," he wrote,

> I am sending you a Christian song, which I sang with a sincere heart in my prison through God's spirit. May the Lord teach you, too, to sing it to his praise and glory. . . .

I thank God for you; I thank my heavenly Father who in his grace gave you to me and united us through his faithful servants. Now I have given you back to him, my chosen gift from God, and with all my heart commend you to the Lord's keeping, along with the children whom he in his grace gave us both. . . .

Where I have wronged you, forgive me for Christ's sake. . . . Greet my dear brother Leonhard Sailer from me and ask him to teach you the tune; sing it for my sake.

Shortly afterward, Jeronimus died together with his two friends – "burned to ashes in Vienna on the Friday before Passion Sunday," as the Hutterite *Chronicle* records.

Traindel Käls must have learned his song, and taught it to her children and to others. Twenty-two years later and six hundred miles away, another Anabaptist, Hans Schmidt, sang it as he was led through the streets of Aachen on the way to his own execution.

Jeronimus' song survived almost five centuries among the descendants of the Anabaptist community to which he belonged. It forms part of the Hutterite songbook that my wife grew up singing from with her family in South Dakota. Today it still teaches new generations the joy of costly discipleship for which its composer lived and died.

The Romantics thought that music can enable us to commune directly with the Absolute – with God. Music can't do that, at least not on its own. But as the story of Jeronimus and his song shows, music does have a power that points to eternal things. It can equip us to face our own mortality with cheerful bravery. And it can draw us into a community in which the living share in the same song as those who have gone before and those yet to be born. That's reason enough to make music. ⤳

Marta Zamarska,
Winter Impression I,
oil on canvas, 2014

Sunrise and Swag

". . . Over and over again we have seen that there is in this country another power than that which has its seat at Westminster."—Clement Attlee

The river sings a duet with the mist
as gulls gavotte around the overflow
and peck at City scum; two Freemen row
across the dawn, five plastic bottles drift
seawards. The river's left the beach undressed
again. A dead rat pitches to and fro
on green-fringed ripples. While the tide is low,
mudlarks mob the shore at hope and sift
frisking the sand for swag, and as the sun
slides pinkly in to light up bankers' reach,
a host of windows seize the light. The gods
command the brokers' choir to rise as one
and sing a song of money: the plundered beach
is deafened as the trading floor applauds.

JACQUELINE SAPHRA

Doing Bach Badly

When our amateur choir sings Bach's Saint Matthew Passion, *the music's power overwhelms our mistakes.*

MAUREEN SWINGER

"**S**EE HIM?" demands Choir One across the space of our meeting hall. "Whom?" calls Choir Two, over the heads of the orchestra, whose bows dip and spike under the returning answer, "The bridegroom, Christ." Four young sopranos softly start the descant, "O Lamb of God, most holy," then realize they need to lift above both choirs and all the woodwinds. Their next line is bolder as the choirs gather intensity in their call-and-response lament. "Come, ye daughters, share my anguish . . . "

Thirty-some instruments and almost one hundred voices in nine parts are deep in the pages of J. S. Bach's *Saint Matthew Passion*. We are so deep that the conductor has lost us, and we stagger to a halt around page eighteen in this first, complex chorus. When you think about it, it's amazing we got this far, considering some in the choir cannot read music, and some in the orchestra have been learning an instrument for just two or three years. Hardly anyone is what you might call professional.

So why is a Bruderhof choir undertaking Bach's greatest oratorio, three hours long, two choirs throughout, almost three hundred years old?

Maureen Swinger is a senior editor at Plough. *She lives at the Fox Hill Bruderhof in Walden, New York, with her husband, Jason, and their three children.*

Opposite: stained glass image of J. S. Bach at the Thomaskirche in Leipzig (modified)

The conductor has lost us, and we stagger to a halt around page eighteen in this first, complex chorus.

We're not complete novices at choral music; the most familiar choruses of Handel's *Messiah* sound forth every Christmas, and occasionally a communal choir has dedicated months toward performances of Camille Saint-Saëns's *Christmas Oratorio* or Joseph Haydn's *Creation*.

The *Saint Matthew Passion*, though, needs its own reckoning. Here there is no ringing "Hallelujah Chorus," no gates flinging wide for the King of Glory, strong and mighty in battle. Every chord, every chorale is taking all participants in one direction – Golgotha.

There are seasons when your soul would like to sidestep, get off the road toward that particular hill on any available back street. But communal gatherings like choir practice are our evening worship services. It's not something you would consider skipping unless you're babysitting small children, or down with the flu. There's also a truly minimal audience

section: perhaps ten chairs for the very elderly, a guest or two, someone with laryngitis. So unless you're really out, you're in.

But you can try to halfway it for a while. From the Choir Two altos I can see a block of high school kids over in Choir One, hunched over, just enduring. "They look like a herd of bison riding out a snowstorm," snorts the alto to my left, and I can't help laughing just a little, but with some sympathy, because, let's face it, I tried the same stunt at their age. Perhaps my generation's parents had a tad more foresight – all of us were assigned confident vocal mentors to sit beside. If I tried the silent slump, my aide responded by holding the book higher and underscoring each word in energetic bursts. You can only manage to ignore such zeal for so long.

My husband Jason is the conductor now. He has no formal training, but his father did it for years, and his grandmother before that. He's a musician and would rather join the orchestra, but somebody has to direct traffic, even if we hardly dare lose our place on the page to glance up and the first violins tend to get ahead of the downbeat.

I know Jason has spent a long time thinking about how to make this practice dynamic and meaningful, keep it flowing while not glossing over the rough patches. But first, a few folks have tips to impart to the young conductor. Even though they're whispering, I know them well enough to guess what's going down.

"In the '70s, the practices used to last for two hours, so we could really drill each part. These Bach harmonies are complex. If we want to be able to sing this piece ten years from now, we need to work hard!" My husband nods.

Next in line: "It's probably wise to keep these practices short and sweet. The high school kids have a lot of homework, and besides, if you want them to have a positive choir experience, don't tax their attention spans." Jason nods again.

He tries to hit the middle ground. "Tenors, let's take this run again; now against the basses; now both choirs, starting at B, with the orchestra." Bach is his favorite composer, so he can't help occasionally pointing out when we might be about to sail past something we shouldn't miss: eleven disciples asking the Lord, in consternation, "Is it I?" then leaving a ringing silence for the twelfth, who knows very well he is the betrayer. Or the way the strings create what composer Leonard Bernstein called a "halo" around every word Jesus speaks, until his final words of desolation on the cross when they go silent and leave him deserted and alone.

For the most part, though, Jason knows the music speaks for itself, and his task is to make sure we are doing it justice. Sometimes that means practicing the pieces out of order; we start by impersonating a furious rabble, scream-singing "His blood be on us and on our children!" and end with a chorale that asks in bewildered pain:

> O Lord, who dares to smite thee,
> as sinful to indict thee,
> deride and mock thee so?
> Thou canst not need confession,
> who knowest not transgression,
> as we and all our children know.

But do we truly know, and what about our children, sitting next to us and holding up the other side of the score? Which part are we really, the mob or the mourners? And if we're standing at the edge of the crowd, observing, there's a cost to that as well.

IN OUR LIVING ROOM LATER, we talk over the practice, as our kids do their homework and listen to their go-to music – not very different from my own teen headphone escapes, truth be told, though they might not believe it. (Will any of that be around in three

Which part are we really, the mob or the mourners? And if we're standing at the edge of the crowd, observing, there's a cost to that as well.

hundred years?) Jason is wondering what to do differently next time; that's when I hear that I guessed right about the whisperers.

What if the comment about teens' attention spans is selling them short? Clearly, for some folks, even ten minutes is too long, but possibly outer limits don't get tested much if they are never reached for. Then again, whether this towering, glorious work finds its way into your heart or not really has little to do with age. I suspect many of us know times when bitterness, anger, or fear freeze out everything the *Passion* communicates. I have sat quietly, pushing the music away, though every chorale speaks of a savior who will never desert us: "To him commit thy ways, who friendless will not leave thee." "His help is nigh to everyone whose faith in him abideth." When the cold

can lay our grief down: with Jesus in the tomb. The original German words by Christian Friedrich Henrici carry all the weight of the world's sorrow. As happens frequently in translation, though, the English in our vocal score deviates from the original by a wide mark, prizing positivity and rhyme over fidelity:

> Here yet awhile, Lord, thou art sleeping,
> Hearts turn to Thee, O Savior blest,
> Rest Thou calmly, calmly rest.
> Death, that holds Thee in its keeping
> When its bonds are loosed by Thee
> Shall become a welcome portal,
> Leading man to life immortal,
> Where he shall Thy glory see.

Those of German heritage in our community considered Bach betrayed, and a few decades ago some of our best linguists started looking for a closer translation for this and several other choruses and arias. They ended up adapting a newer one that came closer to the mood of Henrici's text. The practicalities of the change were onerous, involving yards and yards of white correction tape typed up and hand-applied into a hundred copies, words stretched out to match the eight separate staves of music per page. But the result surely did better justice to what Bach had in mind:

> In tears of grief, dear Lord, we leave thee.
>   Hearts cry to thee, O Savior blest:
> Rest thou softly, softly rest.
>   Rest thy worn and bruised body.
> At thy grave, O Jesu blest,
> May the sinner, worn with weeping,
> Comfort find in thy dear keeping,
> And the weary soul find rest.
> Savior blest, slumber now, and take thy rest.

It isn't time for resurrection yet. The weight of this sacrifice can't be overleapt. Contradictory as it may seem, in that space of death, mourners can be at peace: their grief is with

Why would an opening line invite anyone to share anguish? Who accepts such an invitation?

finally shatters, the message makes sense again. It always did, I just didn't want it to. "From ill do thou defend me; receive me, lead me home." "I would beside my Lord be watching, that evil draw me not astray."

We may be familiar with holding away pain, with building up the cold fronts that ward off feeling. But why would an opening line invite anyone to share anguish? Who accepts such an invitation? Perhaps people who are carrying their own heavy burdens. For friends whose baby was stillborn, for a widow who lost her husband after a long battle with cancer, here is someone who has gone down to death with them. For the couple who has been praying for years to have a child, "Alone thou wilt not leave me, for thou hast tasted grief." Once you have sung or heard these words, they come back to you like an echo in a silent time.

Grief is the language of this work, and the final chorus brings us to the place where we

God. And those who know they have sinned will find redemption.

THOSE WHO KNOW. However, at age fifteen I couldn't be bothered with the concept of sin; surely there was nothing wrong with me. All I knew was that I was stuck in yet another choir practice centered on betrayal and sorrow. If I was having any evil thoughts at all, they were directed at the long-winded choir director who was again belaboring a point that Bach would immediately explain better once the music actually began. Sure enough, those jolting, shuddering cellos did evoke an earthquake. The tenor soloist hit wild, jarring notes. There was the sound of a rending temple veil. On a technical level, I was ready to admit that was cool. Mildly annoyed, mildly impressed, I was completely and thoroughly unprepared for what followed.

For two brief measures, both choirs melded into the voice of the centurion, looking up from the foot of the cross as the realization dawns: "Truly this was the Son of God." It's the most radiant declaration, a wall of sound that reaches from the hill to the heavens, with no way around it. Angels ought to have announced it, but instead, it's an admission by the man responsible for Jesus' death, coming just too late to save him. I could not have been more shocked if I'd been thrown onto the floor.

My earthquake had hit belatedly, and I couldn't regain my footing. At some point I realized the tenor soloist was continuing the story, but how could there be any more to tell? Wretchedly, uselessly mopping up tears with my sleeve, I couldn't read words I suddenly really wanted to see, as the choir laid the Son of God in his tomb:

And now the Lord to rest is laid,
Lord Jesus, rest in peace.

His sorrows o'er, for all our sin
  atonement made,
    Lord Jesus, rest in peace.
O consecrated body, see, with repentant
  tears we would bedew it,
Which our offence to such a death has
  brought.
    Lord Jesus, rest in peace.
While life shall last, let us adore and praise
  the Lord,
That he for man has full redemption
  wrought.
    Lord Jesus, rest in peace.

There must come a point when the ground stops shaking and all of us who had a hand in Christ's death can say, in one voice, "Truly, this was the Son of God."

While life shall last. It's been half a lifetime since that earthquake. It didn't change everything at once. But there is a ground-shift that happens the first time you know – truly know – that God is. Eventually you need to do something about it.

We still practice parts of the *Saint Matthew Passion* almost every year. We don't always have a tenor who dares to sing his way through the earthquake, and if we don't, then the centurion can't speak either. I know it shouldn't matter, when every line and note that Bach wrote is both crucifixion and redemption. Still, there must come a point when the ground stops shaking and all of us who had a hand in Christ's death can say, in one voice, "Truly, this was the Son of God." ➢

Dolly Parton is MAGNIFICENT

The beloved Tennessee singer-songwriter
gets the joke. Do the rest of us?

MARY TOWNSEND

LIKE THE LACONIC WIT OF THE ANCIENT Spartans, American country music and its aesthetic often inspire confusion. The reason for the fringe, stylized leaves, flowers, and animals on the boots, hats, guitars, and epaulettes is at best unclear, and at worst, as my mother would say, tacky. And why would anyone want to sound like that on purpose? The twang, the drawl, the vowels that draw out complicated diphthongs for no apparent reason seem to be a willful commitment to the opposite of smart.

But like the Spartans' abrupt use of language, and their calculated rejection of the more tendentious aspects of Athenian style, there is a canniness and sophistication to country music's appeal to simplicity, once you can catch the joke. Few understand this better than Dolly Parton. On the surface, her grand and rhinestone-laden mode of showmanship is almost inexplicable – until you start to notice that almost everyone seems to admire it. On occasion, some do find the eye-catchingly artificial aspect of Dolly off-putting, or the nostalgic orientation of country in general to be not to their taste. But more often, people who have no commitment to country, and know only a single one of her songs ("Jolene"), like the college students in my ethics classes do, are impressed with her persona in a way that radiates outward through the culture at large. In prison, Nelson Mandela would request "Jolene" the better to pace back

There is a canniness and sophistication to country music's appeal to simplicity, once you can catch the joke.

and forth; my son sings "Jolene" on the way to school. My grandmother, herself a petite woman with a penchant for grandly styled hair, owned a white Cadillac not unlike the one on the cover of Dolly's 1989 album *White Limozeen*; my father remembers her playing Dolly's first album on their blue portable turntable every Saturday morning.

There is an uncanny strength to the spirit with which people praise Dolly Parton. It seems those who love Dolly aren't just fans, they love her with their whole souls.

The narrowness of musical genre would ordinarily seem to prohibit the kind of universal love Dolly Parton attracts, yet her shows continue to gather people from all sorts of political backgrounds and locales. Americans got a new taste of the magnetism of this emotion when the news of Dolly's million-dollar donation to vaccine research hit in 2020 – an unusual pleasure, in the midst of the chaos, to have someone so lovable to thank.

NPR's radio series *Dolly Parton's America* considers whether the idea that her careful retention of such a broad audience can be ascribed to virtues of showmanship, business acumen, and an ability to deflect political questioning. But I think there's more to it than that, in a way that sets my philosophical instincts buzzing. Dolly Parton is not simply a good person, or a beautiful poetess; she is both beautiful and good, in a way the philosophy of character strives to explain but can't always illustrate convincingly. Usually, our heroes disappoint us with flaws or scandal, or our admiration and interest wanes and we move on to the next person to admire. But the more I come to learn about Dolly, the stronger my feelings become. When I told my students the Nelson Mandela story, it made their day.

Mary Townsend is an assistant professor of philosophy at St. John's University. She is the author of The Woman Question in Plato's Republic, *and her articles have also appeared in the* Hedgehog Review.

DOLLY PARTON WAS born into poverty in Tennessee's Smoky Mountains. There was no electricity; in the winter everyone slept in their clothes. Her father was a Pentecostal preacher and her mother spoke in tongues; everyone sang and played anything that came to hand. Her whole family was musical; she wrote songs with her evangelist aunt, and her uncle drove her to Nashville when she was eighteen. Her voice, a perfectly pitched soprano, seems to leap past her to resonate everywhere at once. Of her sixty-five albums, forty-four have been in the top ten on the country charts. Dolly has written more than three thousand songs. When her early fame seemed in danger of plateauing during the years she worked with television star and singer Porter Wagoner, who behind the scenes was combative, controlling, and just plain jealous, she sang her way out of the situation by composing the song "I Will Always Love You" on the very same day she wrote "Jolene." That she did love or would always love Porter was not an uncomplicatedly true sentiment, as you can see from her visible discomfort in the 1974 video of her singing the song on Porter's show. But as musical politesse, it was enough to get her off the hook gracefully, and on to better things.

All this speaks to a great talent. But what she did with her fame and the resulting fortune shows her character. Dolly created a global literacy program in honor of her father, who never learned to read. She has made a substantial investment in her rural community via her theme park, Dollywood (which includes, of all things, a highly successful bald eagle sanctuary). With royalties from Whitney Houston's cover of "I Will Always Love You," Dolly has also invested in a Black neighborhood in Nashville. And then there's the medical fund in honor of the doctor who delivered her, who worked for their community for almost nothing, among many other acts of generosity and recognition of her roots.

But even as the sum of the parts, these facts and deeds don't really capture what is so compelling about Dolly. We love her, but usually love isn't this inarticulate. Being a philosophy professor, my impulse is to turn to the nearest philosopher at hand. But it may be that Dolly can do more to explain the philosophers than the other way around. Let us make a start, however, with Aristotle's understanding of human character and what he notices about this precise kind of wordlessness of praise. Be warned that Aristotle won't be entirely able to wrap his head around the idea that a petite woman with a high voice might be a profound moral exemplar.

Dolly Parton, age five, with her family in 1951

Photograph by Nancy Barr Brandon. Used by permission.

Photograph by Richard E. Aaron. Used by permission.

I spend a fair amount of time looking for ways to make the philosophy of character interesting to undergraduates. This is surprisingly difficult, or perhaps unsurprisingly, since we often think of goodness as something pedestrian, tired, a bit of a burden. My students would rather die than admit this to me, however, and so we often find ourselves at loggerheads, I myself struggling to explain why this foundational aspect of our lives is relevant at all, while they remain constitutionally committed to remaining cheery and upbeat about something they obviously find boring.

I usually save Aristotle's *Nicomachean Ethics* for the end of the semester, in part because it allows students to discover with relief that he's more sensible than many of the other people we read. But I also do this because of what he adds to the conversation: a single untranslatable word, *kalos*, which in English we can only weakly translate as "noble" or

"fine" or with the better but still not adequate "beautiful." *Kalos* describes something that is good but also lovely, perfectly beautiful while astonishingly good, the kind of thing to aim for in word and deed that would never be boring, tired, or pedestrian; never merely a duty but always a pleasure.

Whenever we humans manage to act really excellently – in a sense not at all unlike the *Bill and Ted's Excellent Adventure* sense of "excellent" – we do so only when the reason *why* we do the thing we do is because it is beautiful; in this way we catch at something like happiness, at least according to Aristotle – not to mention his biggest fan, Thomas Aquinas. But if we, stuck in the language of twenty-first-century America, don't happen to have a familiar word for the goal our actions ought to aim for, we are likely to have trouble figuring out what to do with ourselves and our lives, as we obviously do. And so, when someone proposes that Aristotle's philosophy has something to tell us that later thinkers in other languages lack, we find his suggestion that in order to be happy we ought to act more "virtuously" rather hollow. Fortunately for us, this is where Dolly Parton comes in.

FROM THE VERY BEGINNING, Dolly had a natural sort of relation to her talent and the ambition that carried her into stardom. She wrote her first song when she was six, performed publicly at age ten. She talks about always knowing she could make a rhyme whenever she wanted. Her grandmother took her on the bus to Lake Charles, Louisiana (my hometown, and the hometown of my own grandmother) to make her first record; they got a bit lost and almost didn't make it, but people gave them food to keep them going, and Dolly worked up the courage to ask for directions. In all this, Dolly displays a quality Aristotle describes as seriousness: not some kind of already-achieved perfection, but the kind of commitment to one's desire that it takes to keep walking toward the beautiful. Our human relation to virtue or excellence, Aristotle contends, is our proper serious work, much like the way serious harp players work hard and well at their music. Reading too quickly, sometimes this argument sounds like he's saying the work of the human is to be good at their career. But our work at our job, even a job we have a genius for, pales in comparison to the human work we must do on behalf of our souls; and Dolly's tenacity does not stop at her ambition.

While no one works harder at prudential care for her musical legacy than Dolly (she already has an album ready to be released the year after her death), the work of her heart is more magnificent still. Per Aristotle, magnificent acts must be aimed at the common good, not the individual's own luxury or aura of power, and this is the hallmark of all of Dolly's projects, from vaccines to bald eagles; and unlike the Carnegies with their libraries, or the Rockefellers with their ice-skating rink, there is no large-scale rapaciousness to make up for, either.

When her colleagues in music and entertainment start to talk about Dolly, they acknowledge without reservation not only her talent and business sense, but also her possession of genuine human decency, her kindness, justice, and sweetness. But there's also a piquancy to the way Dolly tells the truth that does not cut corners. In her ballads, taking on the personae of hundreds of women, she tells about murder ("J. J. Sneed"), suicide ("The Bridge"), madness ("Where Beauty Lives in Memory"), adultery ("You're the One Who Taught Me How to Swing"), starving children ("Little Andy") – all the anguish of things

that people in her town and in her family experienced. In her 2020 memoir *Dolly Parton, Songteller: My Life in Lyrics*, she speaks of her ability to articulate what people in these situations might want to explain but cannot. Her song about retirement homes is called "House of Shame." But this honesty also arrives in the ordinary moments of any given day. In the 2019 documentary *Here I Am*, Dolly recounts to an audience of rapt Londoners in 1983 how she responded in kind to someone who'd flipped her off earlier in the day, asking with wicked innocence, "Did I do that right?" While Loretta Lynn had her 1966 hit with the all-too-understandable title "You Ain't Woman Enough (To Take My Man)," Dolly's account of the man-stealing Jolene is based on admiration of Jolene's own beauty and virtues, rather than jealousy. And if there can be said to be a virtue of the erotic, Dolly has that too: married with real faithfulness to her husband, Carl Dean, for more than fifty-five years, she nevertheless manages to express human appreciation for the opposite sex, even as an older woman. As seen in the glorious 1989 music video of "Why'd You Come in Here Looking Like That" from *White Limozeen*, a song my grandmother and I listened to on the radio, Dolly's narration jokingly critiques the choice of cowboy men to dress too attractively; in the music video, she makes clear with a well-timed wolf whistle her universal appreciation, with, nevertheless, a certain restraint.

For Aristotle, kalos describes something that is good but also lovely, perfectly beautiful while astonishingly good; never merely a duty but always a pleasure.

To all this, Dolly adds bravado. Recounting her reasons for not being scared to perform live even at a very young age, or to begin a career in the knives-out, male-dominated space of Nashville, Dolly remarks, "And I didn't care. I wasn't scared of anybody. I mean, what was you gonna do to me, kill me? And if you kill me, what you gonna do, eat me?" In the 1980 film *9 to 5*, we see Dolly's character, based on herself, confronting and threatening with castration the boss who'd tried to make a move on her; she's quite convincing. The song she wrote after she finally broke with the abusive Porter, "Light of a Clear Blue Morning," speaks to a similar triumph; hitting the stamp-clap downbeat in gospel style, she compares herself to an eagle ready for the sky. The chorus keeps repeating again in stronger, tighter, faster loops, that "everything's going to be all right / everything's going to be OK." Dolly offers her own courage to us as well, in a way that leaps out past the record to encourage the heart.

Listening to Whitney Houston, Dolly felt joy that her song had become more than it started out as, and that it had lifted up another woman.

Finally, there is the sort of heroic generosity it takes to recognize outstanding virtue in other people. Whitney Houston's version of "I Will Always Love You" first came out in November 1992, when I was eleven. For a few months, it was as though no other song existed. One heard it everywhere – on the radio, people singing it to each other in the hallways of school – and not a soul felt it was overplayed. At an intrastate competition in Lafayette, Louisiana, no fewer than three young girls sang it as their competition piece, and one of them won. When Dolly first heard it on the radio, she recounts that she had to pull the car off the road and stop until it was done. Whitney has the treble register no less than Dolly but resonates from even more of her frame, and the power of her whole soul transforms the careful détente of Dolly's duplicitous version from eighteen years before into an extraordinary testament of love and renunciation at its full cost. The independence that Dolly bought the hard way with the song is transformed by Whitney into an anthem that contains more human beauty than Dolly could initially let herself express on stage, even though that power was present in the songwriting from the beginning. While some songwriters might be envious at this contrast, what Dolly felt was joy that her song had become more than it started out as, and that it had lifted up another woman. She feels this way about many of her creations; as she reflects in *Songteller*, she can think of song after song that could one day be a bigger hit for someone else.

NE PERENNIAL HUMAN obstacle to virtue, Aristotle observes, is that most of us think rather less of ourselves than we ought – a surprising sentiment to hear from the otherwise solidly self-loving pagan world. For if the pagans can't appreciate themselves, how on earth will we? We are capable of more than we give ourselves credit for, he says, and when we decide with much grinding of soul to stand aside from the sorts of projects and honors we are more than capable of carrying off, we are, as he puts it, small-souled. Of course, people who overestimate what they can do or have done are vain. But there are those who are capable of great things and know it, and it would be wiser of humanity, flirting not so much with proper humility but with self-humiliation, to aim toward something more like this state of greatness, toward largeness, toward expansiveness of being. To do so is to have *megalopsychia* – to have, literally, a large soul.

Now, who ever ran across a person more capable of great things, and who *knew* this capability, than Dolly Parton? Here is goodness that one could never accuse of being pedestrian. Her very hair is explicable on these grounds. Larger than life, it announces her before she arrives, and signals that someone has at last understood the proper task of the human, to reach out with all our hearts toward the divine in the ways that we humanly can.

Being a star, as Dolly points out, is not so much about the existence of a large number of fans as it is a state of mind, a feeling in one's own heart about one's self. This is exactly the sort of graceful and accurate reckoning of one's self and one's great deeds that Aristotle describes. Of course, Dolly will speak humbly of her talents, or of her business sense, to let us know that being great-souled hasn't gone to her head. Properly speaking, there's always an element of what we would call humility in great-souledness, since one's estimation of one's self has to be perfectly calibrated; even a smidgeon of overestimation would spoil the whole.

Even for the pagan Aristotle, there has to be a sense that as great as one is, one is nevertheless not a god. A Christian must take it a step further to recognize that she is, like anyone else, "a poor sinful creature," as Dolly put it in her 1975 song "The Seeker." Aquinas remarks that the great-souled

Christian deems himself worthy of great things in consideration of the gifts he holds from God; and while humility reminds us to honor the way others live up to their own great gifts, magnanimity reminds us that not to live up to greatness is to disrespect what has been given. Although Dolly's theological sense would never please a Thomist, there's a charity present in all her works that vivifies the notion that such love is the mother and the root of all virtues, the very sort of love that magnanimity reaches out towards and attempts to perfect, as much as is humanly possible.

DOLLY CONFOUNDS and yet fulfills Aristotle's ideal in more ways than one. In Aristotle's description of great-souledness, he gets surprisingly specific about the physical attributes of the human being in possession of this sort of singular virtue. It becomes explicit that the person he's imagining is a very male sort of man. Arguing that nothing small can be beautiful, Aristotle concludes that the

Recalling her father's illiteracy, Dolly launched the Imagination Library in 1995, providing each registered child with one free book per month. Since then the program has expanded to include nearly two million children across five countries.

Photograph from Daily Mirror/Mirrorpix/Mirrorpix via Getty Images. Used by permission.

Initially great-souledness seems reasonable enough, insofar as knowledge of one's abilities is always useful; but on consideration it seems to put its possessor in an impossible, even ridiculous place in relation to other people – and in relation to one's unalterable personal proportions. One might ask what one is to do if one wishes for greatness while being short, female, with a high sort of voice, and a propensity for moving quickly. Possibly put on a wig and high heels, for starts, but also figure out how to reconcile oneself toward other human beings in light of the friendly love that even pagan Aristotle thinks we can't help having toward any given member of the human species.

In fact, the humorous grandeur of Dolly's ever-so-slightly trashy aesthetic both elevates and humanizes her. When asked point-blank by Barbara Walters if the goofiness of her hair, makeup, and costumes make her into a joke, Dolly fired back:

> I've often made the statement that I would never stoop so low as to be fashionable; that's the easiest thing in the world to do. So I just decided that I would do something that would at least get the attention. Once they got past the shock of the ridiculous way I looked and all that, then they would see that there was parts of me to be appreciated. And show business is a money-making joke. And I've just always liked telling jokes, you know.

To stay afloat so gracefully amid the commercialism of such a performing life, one might well find it necessary to feel a sort of great-souled contempt for certain aspects of it. But Dolly has transcended the need for contempt by means of a certain kind of irony. As she points out, her costuming is a very specific kind of joke about the awkwardness of such a

great-souled man will need to be tall, to walk slowly in his dignity, and possess a deep or heavy voice. Now, it's odd to place such weight on external qualities when, after all, this virtue is explicitly about the soul and the soul's relation to its invisible qualities. Some readers have argued that there's even a humorous aspect to his description, since the great-souled man begins his life in search of honor and respect from others, and ends by having such a low opinion for the lesser souls he encounters as to be comically contemptuous. On these grounds, it would be hard to imagine such a man having many friends, since for Aristotle friends are necessarily analogous to each other in excellence, and this man would be without equals. But a life without friends, as Aristotle reminds us, seems hardly worth living, and so one has to ask how good a life such a great man would really have.

relation to the public, made because it allows her to set others at ease.

Casual critics might at first assume there must not be much in the head of a human being with such a busty flamboyance of style. But once they are moved past this reaction to notice the real goodness of her performance and indeed her soul, their estimation can rise to a more accurate level, and participate in the joke at the expense of their confusion. In this way, with a sort of Socratic irony of wigs, Dolly dissembles her greatness while also showing it off. It's a masterpiece of showmanship and of excellence that Aristotle's slow-moving man simply could not achieve. It also illustrates Aristotle's contention that great-souledness ornaments the virtues: Dolly ornaments herself with a dash of irony in order to render her virtues visible, and in this way her great-souledness gathers not our envy but our love.

WHEN WE TURN in the twenty-first century to Aristotle's description of what it would take to make real human happiness for ourselves, we know we need to recover the *kalos* thing that thinkers like Aquinas and even Augustine had more graceful access to. But one thing we tend to get immediately wrong is that we translate Aristotle's careful, open-ended dialectic into firm pronouncements on virtue, where if we work hard and have good habits, we'll perforce be happy. Aristotle's philosophy is smarter than that: we remain at the mercy of chance for many of the things that make up not just happiness but our ability to make our way toward excellence in the first place. We are at the mercy of the family who raises us, having enough food, and the trust in having food enough for tomorrow that allows the mind to deliberate and choose. Aristotle therefore asks us to see the difference between a life of blessedness, where someone has an abundance of the good things of life and the virtue to manage them well, and the more precarious happiness where most of us land, the place where we hope for more food, more courage, and more ability to love tomorrow.

And when we do run across the human being who has achieved a sort of escape velocity from the toil of being almost virtuous but not yet, we remain in an odd sort of position toward her, once we try to reckon with the sheer magnitude of her life in relation to ours.

There are simply some people, Aristotle insists, who exceed our ability to praise them, to articulate what their extraordinary virtue would mean to ourselves.

This is the truth of Dolly Parton's magnificence. We can't simply praise her. But we can, as Aristotle puts it, bless her – sort of raise our eyes in astonishment, wonder, and gratitude that a human being could be so beautifully good. It's our luck that this human being is not tucked away in some distant estate or time, but a living performer whose records and music we can turn to any time we need a human example of virtue to pick us up. Dolly's goodness is beautiful. You could never for a second suspect it of being boring. What is virtue, what is the good, what is the beautiful? It looks a little like Dolly Parton. The joke's on us if we miss the point of her remarkable life. ⇌

> *With a sort of Socratic irony of wigs, Dolly dissembles her greatness while also showing it off.*

Go Tell It on

Black spirituals aren't just for Black churches.
They should be sung by everyone.

STEPHEN MICHAEL NEWBY

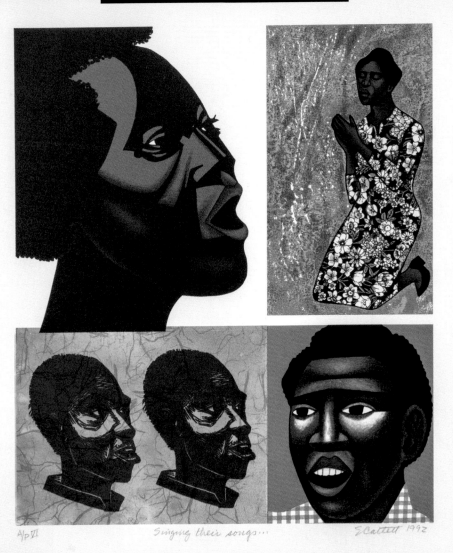

the Mountain

IT'S CHRISTMAS EVE 2021, and here I am, a descendant of enslaved Africans, leading my predominantly White Presbyterian congregation in Atlanta, Georgia, in singing the Black spiritual "Go Tell It on the Mountain." The song is not being presented to the congregation as a performance concert piece. Instead, I've prepared an arrangement that allows it to be what it was always meant to be: a relational, transformative, communal act of worship that joins us together.

My great-grandfather six generations removed, Michael, who was enslaved less than a hundred miles from here in Jones County, Georgia, would never have imagined such a picture. I am deeply moved and thankful for this moment in time and how far we have come.

Three years before I arrived at this church, I visited the Jones County archives to research my ancestry. I found the graves of the Newby family, the White landowners in the area. I stood in front of a Newby tombstone, fists clenched and heart grieved, imagining all that my ancestors had suffered at this man's hands. The sun was shining brightly. Even the mosquitoes were quiet. At that moment God spoke into my heart and said, "Be reconciled."

I had already spent three decades trying to bridge divides by bringing different genres of music into conversation. But now this call to live out reconciliation with others would lead me to share my people's music with predominantly White congregations throughout the United States and particularly here in the South. Whatever our personal histories, I can think of no better way to express our shared longing for liberation from the bonds of racism than the spirituals.

THE SPIRITUALS, rich with historical, theological, and social nuance, come down to us from enslaved Africans. Many will have heard that the enslaved used spirituals to communicate messages to one another that their oppressors would not recognize. Biblical stories and theological themes often masked an underlying message: the song "Go Down, Moses" was not just about the biblical figure but was sung to signal people to prepare themselves to flee north toward freedom. Another song, "Follow the Drinking Gourd," literally gave directions for how to navigate northward by following the North Star. When spirituals referred to Satan, that could be code for the slave master. Songs about Jesus' crucifixion were also about the lynchings happening within their own communities. Only those in the community would be able to recognize these encoded messages, sung right under the noses of the slave owners.

But there's more to it than that. While the hardships of slavery, and the enslaved people's

Opposite: Elizabeth Catlett, *Singing Their Songs,* lithograph on paper, 1992

Stephen Michael Newby is director of the Center for African American Worship Studies at Trevecca Nazarene University in Nashville, minister of worship at Peachtree Presbyterian Church in Atlanta, and a professor of music at Seattle Pacific University.

Elizabeth Catlett, *Walking Blindly*, lithograph on paper, 1992

In his 2004 history of Black gospel music, *People Get Ready!*, Robert Darden writes that when the enslaved were taken from their homelands and communities in Africa, there was something that the slave owners could not strip from them. They may have been language-impoverished because they were deprived of literacy, but they could pass on their stories through work songs, spirituals, and dance. Darden points out another fascinating aspect of the spirituals: there seems in them to be no sense of historical time lapse. It is as if the singers have such a deeply personal relationship with the biblical characters that they sing directly to them.

STANDING AT THE NEWBY GRAVE, I could not escape this calling to bring people together in radical racial reconciliation through singing. I had been conducting multiethnic musical groups for thirty years, musically and spiritually sojourning, discovering the beauty of diversity as one of God's gifts to creation. Gathering to sing under the auspices of unity brings all those involved into a space I describe as a "mutuality of grace." When we sing in harmony, we become more aware of the grace that holds all creation together. We engage holistically, connecting with everyone in the room as we focus on blending our sound, adding to the collective voice.

Although I didn't know where it would lead at the time, I stumbled upon racial reconciliation through singing as a graduate student at the University of Massachusetts at Amherst in 1986. For my master's thesis I composed a multiethnic, intergenerational oratorio entitled *Be Still and Know.* I was interested in blending gospel music and jazz in the context of theater. I grew up in a strict Missionary Baptist

expectations of freedom, are evident all over the spirituals, they carry significance for us as well. These are universal songs about heaven and hell, and about our spiritual captivity and liberation, that ring true far beyond their specific historical context.

The spirituals endure to this day because they are creatively and beautifully crafted songs with undeniably powerful melodies and semantics. Though now they are often sung in a minor key, historical studies suggest that while most spirituals incorporated minor chords, they consisted primarily of major chords. Their originality is evident not just in the way the music is structured, but in the way it affects listeners. The rhythm is off the typical beat, in a way that naturally gives rise to bodily movement, inviting people to be involved in more than just a song. Perhaps this more than anything separates Black music from the hymns that White Christians were singing in church.

tradition where playing jazz was not supported in the context of church. I was unfamiliar with the sacred services commissioned by the Episcopal archdiocese of San Francisco from Duke Ellington in 1965. But deep within my consciousness I knew there was a connection between jazz and gospel and the spirituals. I knew that fusing diverse musical elements creates something new and positive, not only in our music but in our humanity. And I knew my ancestors had practiced fusing cultures as a means of surviving and thriving.

Already at this early stage in my musical-spiritual formation, I dreamed about bringing together people from what I might call contra-puntal musical narratives. I asked myself what would happen if, among all the racial division in Detroit and its suburbs, we could get White folks and Black folks to sing together. I decided to pursue the idea by holding gospel music workshops with churches from inner-city Detroit, the surrounding suburbs, and Ann Arbor. For more than ten years we had ten to fifteen churches coming together to practice racial reconciliation through singing. We visited each other's churches. We broke bread together. We fellowshipped and built friendships that have held strong to this day.

In *The Spirituals and the Blues* (1972), James H. Cone describes the spirituals as "community music." Singing community music we find ourselves living in community. I believe singing spirituals allows us to transcend cultures of vitriol and racism and ascend toward citizenship in God's kingdom. As the spiritual suggests, "all God's children got shoes" – we are all equal in essence even if we have different roles. When we sing our part in the great symphony of the spirituals, we transcend negativity and live together in harmony in a way that envisions God's kingdom. Singing spirituals takes us to the mountaintop. They help us realize that all of us have been born into an oppressed state of sinfulness and that Jesus Christ lifts us up to receive the liberation God offers to all humanity.

Singing "go tell it on the mountain" on Christmas Eve reminded me of Psalm 133, the "song of ascents" that begins, "How good and pleasant it is when God's people live together in unity!" Speaking of this psalm, Walter Brueggemann writes, "The poem anticipates the solidarity and harmony of all humanity as it lives without defensiveness in a creation benevolent enough to care for all." In the same way, "Go Tell It on the Mountain," reflecting the heart-language of the enslaved, invites us to join in solidarity with all creation as we live out God's liberating kingdom here on earth. The gates of hell shall not prevail against God's kingdom when, singing these songs of liberation and unity under the power of God's spirit, we make a decision to ascend with Christ and to rise above cultures of disunity.

Scripture commands us to teach and admonish one another with psalms, hymns, and spiritual songs (Col. 3:16). Whatever our hermeneutics, theological constructs, or biblical interpretations might be, we can glorify God through these songs. Whether we're Black, White, Hispanic, Asian, whatever our ethnicity or identity, when we sing the songs of those who have been enslaved, we join them in looking for liberation from being enslaved by racism.

I believe we all bleed red and that's the color of reconciliation. Christ shed his blood on Calvary to reconcile all creation to our Heavenly Father. When God's people sing Black spirituals together, we identify with our deep sense of humanity, and we will want to live our lives in ways that help eradicate racism. We sing a song of ascent. We rise above our proclivities and sit in heavenly places, becoming aware that our citizenship is heaven-bound and that we must "sing and bring down" heaven to earth. ➤

In Search *of* Eternity

Why learn to play music if we're all going to die?

EUGENE VODOLAZKIN

In Soviet Ukraine in 1979, Gleb Yanovsky, a fourteen-year-old guitar prodigy, drops out of music school after witnessing a young girl drown. The following excerpt is taken from Eugene Vodolazkin's forthcoming novel Brisbane *(Plough, May 2022).*

GLEB'S FATHER FYODOR found out that he had quit music school. With some delay, a few months later, but he did. And got upset. It was a surprise for everyone who remembered how reserved he'd been about his son's decision to study music. For the first time in years Fyodor asked his ex-wife Irina if they could meet. Hearing that Gleb had abandoned music in view of the death that awaits each of us, Fyodor became agitated and said that this was the act of a genuine musician. That the distinguishing trait of a musician was not the dexterity of his fingers but the constant thought of death, which should instill us with optimism, not horror. Meant to mobilize, not paralyze. "*In other words, true creativity must balance between life and death,*" Fyodor summed up. "*It has to see a little beyond the horizon.*"* But this was only the beginning of the conversation. The actual conversation took place later – and not with Fyodor but with his father Mefody, who had come from Kamianets-Podilskyi to visit his son. Mefody was tall, broad-shouldered, and gray, kind of like Turgenev. The resemblance was heightened because, unlike Fyodor, his grandfather switched to Russian once in a while. And although his language might not have been Turgenevian, his readiness to speak it was much more important. To his grandmother's question of what he thought of Mefody from their first meeting, Gleb said without thinking: well-meaning. The definition was exceptionally precise. Mefody meant well with every word he spoke. With every wrinkle, one might say, of which his face had many. Tiny ones spread around his eyes like a cast net, but there were also large ones as deep as trenches traced from his bridge to the corners of his mouth. Yes, Fyodor wanted the boy to meet his grandfather, but he himself hadn't anticipated that this would be the start of a long-standing friendship. Gleb wouldn't let Mefody go for a minute. It's hard to say what this was: a longing for male company, which Gleb had been deprived of, or the qualities of his grandfather himself. Most likely this was

about his grandfather, since life without a father hadn't nudged Gleb toward his own father. Yes, sometimes Gleb wished he could make an impression on his father, but he had no desire for constant communication. With his grandfather, though, he did. His grandfather turned out to be gentle and easygoing. Unexpectedly, Gleb played the part of grandfather in the interactions between these two people. He led Mefody through his favorite streets and told him about them. His grandfather was a grateful listener. Listening to Gleb, he would nod, but at the end of the story sometimes would ask a question or two that made it clear he knew a lot more about the subject than Gleb. "So you know everything," Gleb said with slow amazement. "*Come now.*" His grandfather gave him a funny blank look as he switched to Ukrainian. "*I don't know anything.*" "Yes, you do!" Gleb would say playfully. One time his grandfather didn't try to vindicate himself and said, "If there's something I definitely do not know, it's why you quit music school." Caught flat-footed, Gleb fell silent. Then he repeated what he'd already said once: "Because I'm going to die." Uttered the first time, those words had been hot, like breath, but now suddenly they seemed like cardboard. Not to

All artwork by Erin Hanson

Eugene Vodolazkin's novel Laurus *won Russia's Big Book Award and the Yasnaya Polyana Book Award. His novel* Brisbane *was translated from the Russian and Ukrainian by Marian Schwartz.*

*Italics indicate Ukrainian is being spoken.

Mefody, though. To Gleb's great surprise, his grandfather considered this line of thinking natural and even praised the boy for his philosophical approach to life. But he didn't forget Gleb's words. They surfaced a few days later, when grandfather and grandson were sitting by the fountain in Zolotovoritska Park. "*If you're going to die,*" Mefody said thoughtfully, "*then why should you go to that music school?*" Gleb heard new notes in the question and so nodded cautiously. His grandfather stood up from the bench, moved closer to the fountain, and put his large hands under the stream. When they were full, he washed his face. He turned back to Gleb. "*But what if you're not going to die?*" "How's that?" Gleb asked. Mefody's face took on a puzzling expression: "There's this idea . . . " Gleb looked at his grandfather and smiled. An idea. That's what a progressive grandfather he had, then. Progressive and even in a way sophisticated. Mefody waved and a taxi stopped in front of them. Like a fairytale! In the blink of an eye! Handsomely. A Volga GAZ-24, which Gleb had never ridden in before. He'd only ridden in a Volga GAZ-21, which Fyodor talked about often, saying it wasn't quite a tank but it wasn't quite a car either. The taxi Gleb's magician-grandfather seated him in had a quiet engine and a smooth ride. His grandfather did

> His grandfather did in fact remind him of a fairytale character because the waves of his hands produced things he'd never seen before.

in fact remind him of a fairytale character because the waves of his hands produced things he'd never seen before. A small church popped up by the Holosiiv Forest as from the sleeve of Vasilisa the Wise, and in that small church, Father Pyotr – fair hair gathered into a bun, neat beard, eyeglasses. The church was straight out of a fairytale, but Father Pyotr more than likely wasn't. He smelled of eau de toilette, and it was obvious that, unlike folklore characters, Father Pyotr took care of himself. After he and Mefody embraced, Mefody smelled of eau de toilette too. Observing these dissimilar men, Gleb realized they were linked if not by personal friendship then by firm, long-standing acquaintance. Mefody told Father Pyotr that his grandson had discovered death for himself, and this, understandably, had made him give up music school. Father Pyotr also found this act natural, inasmuch as what in fact did anyone need music school for if everything was ending in we-know-what. Once he'd received Father Pyotr's approval, Mefody noted that, on the other hand, it was too bad the boy had given up school. Yes, perhaps it was too bad, Father Pyotr agreed, since music links the school to eternity, after all. "Is music eternity?" Gleb asked. Father Pyotr shook his head. "Music is not eternity. But it reminds us of eternity – profound music does." "What is eternity?" Gleb

> Music is not eternity. But it reminds us of eternity – profound music does.

asked. "It is the absence of time," Mefody conjectured, "which means the absence of death." "Ultimately it is God," Father Pyotr said. "The One you are seeking." The priest gave Gleb a New Testament, a catechism, and a prerevolutionary textbook, *Divine Law*. In parting, he asked him to learn the Symbol of Faith, which was marked in the textbook with a piece of velvet. When he got home, Gleb put the three books in front of him and read them in turn. One of them (*Divine Law*) he took to school the next day. Sitting in his social studies class, he read it under the desk. His teacher, walking along the rows, silently stole up from behind and plucked the book from Gleb's lap. To general laughter, she read the title, and her first reaction was surprise. That was not what she expected to find in a lap under a desk. She opened the book to the bookmark and tried to read it out loud and stumbled. Obviously, knowledge of social studies was inadequate for that kind of reading. She closed the book. "So, maybe we go to church?" she asked Gleb. The first person plural, it occurred to Gleb, how self-centered. Not only would he not have gone with her to church, he wouldn't even have gone with her to . . . She came right up to him and inquired, "Do we pray and beat our brows?" Gleb tried to snatch the book from his teacher's hands, but she deftly turned away. "Do we beat our brows?" she asked again. "That's none of your

business," Gleb snarled. "That is where you are mistaken, Yanovsky. It is my business and the business of the Young Communist organization, if, of course, you are a Young Communist." Gleb actually did belong to the Young Communists. At first he hadn't planned to join, but Fyodor called that step a bad omen. From his observations, those who didn't join the Young Communists later did not get into university or conservatory. During the break, the social studies specialist took the Young Communist member to see the principal, an elderly, good-natured lady. Placing *Divine Law* on her desk, the teacher said, "Here is what our school's Young Communists are reading. Young Communist Pilgrims." Leafing through the book, the principal thanked the teacher for her vigilance, and this gratitude, it seemed to Gleb, was not without irony, as the "You may go" tossed casually to the social studies specialist attested. The elderly lady did not believe in God but did not like tattle-tales. She decided not to complicate Gleb's future and so limited herself to an informational conversation. The principal directed Gleb's attention to the fact that Gagarin flew into outer space but did not see God. From this, it seemed to her, followed the inescapable conclusion that there is no God. She asked that someone from the Yanovsky family come to pick up his *Divine Law* – which was a mild summons to the school. The boy gave this a couple of days' thought and then reasoned that the best thing to do in this case was go to his grandfather. After all, the confiscated book, ultimately, had come through him. When Gleb told Mefody what had happened, he showed no concern whatsoever. He only asked whether Gleb had managed to memorize the Symbol of Faith. No. That's fine, too (his grandfather smiled), maybe now the principal will. He asked his grandson for a piece of paper and in a calligraphic hand wrote the Symbol of Faith on it. He explained

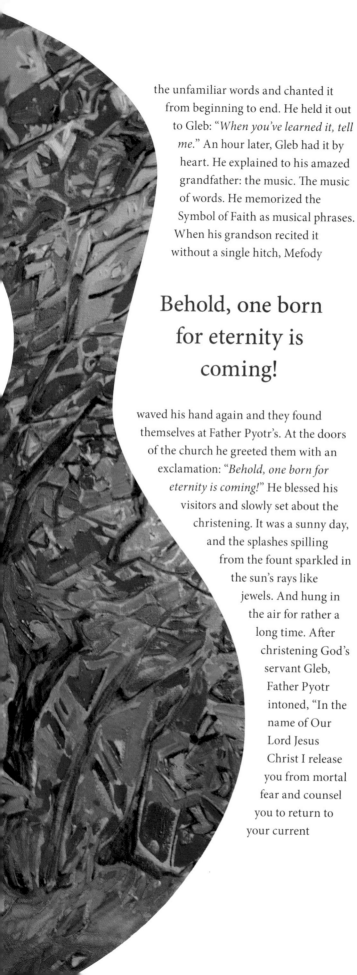

the unfamiliar words and chanted it from beginning to end. He held it out to Gleb: *"When you've learned it, tell me."* An hour later, Gleb had it by heart. He explained to his amazed grandfather: the music. The music of words. He memorized the Symbol of Faith as musical phrases. When his grandson recited it without a single hitch, Mefody

Behold, one born for eternity is coming!

waved his hand again and they found themselves at Father Pyotr's. At the doors of the church he greeted them with an exclamation: *"Behold, one born for eternity is coming!"* He blessed his visitors and slowly set about the christening. It was a sunny day, and the splashes spilling from the fount sparkled in the sun's rays like jewels. And hung in the air for rather a long time. After christening God's servant Gleb, Father Pyotr intoned, "In the name of Our Lord Jesus Christ I release you from mortal fear and counsel you to return to your current

affairs – for example, to your studies at the music school. Work, my friend, to the glory of God! While remembering that eternity lies ahead, do not neglect time, for only in time can something be achieved. Your parents asked that you not be registered in the church book to avoid problems with our militantly atheistic state – and so I am not registering you. Know that you are registered with the Lord, and that is what is most important. In difficult moments, rely on me and on your grandfather Mefody." At these words, the newly christened young man remembered that Mefody had before him his meeting with the principal, and his heart sank. He worried in vain, however. The eldest in the Yanovsky clan took full responsibility for his assignment and headed for school the very next day. Mefody's gray hair made the most favorable impression on the principal, who began her conversation with him with what seemed to her an irrefutable argument. Returning the confiscated book to Gleb's grandfather, she took him by the elbow rather theatrically and led him to the window. Pointing to the sky, she said, *"Yuri Gagarin flew in space but did not see God. You agree?"* Mefody politely bowed his head: *"True, Yuri Gagarin did not see God."* Not tearing himself away from the sky in the window, the old man smiled broadly. *"But God saw him. And blessed him."*

Marta
Zamarska,
Misty Rails,
batik (paint
and hot wax
on fabric),
2008

Poland, 1985

And the façades of Warsaw bared
their scrubbed-up skins; liveried waiters

offered nothing on the menu; bath water
rusted; the country roads were calm,

a past I sought long overgrown,
the state of currency still volatile,

human traces vague, all guesses wild.
Nothing left to find; nothing and no one.

But oh, the language: soft-tongued,
apologetic; those legends of tracks

pointing towards infinity; haystacks,
horse-drawn carts; disappearing villages

where elders with wizened sensibilities,
surely hungry for redemption, would

offer water, sanctuary and bread.
Perhaps they remembered. Perhaps

going about their rural business
they thought of all those trains; night

and day, the passing of human freight.
But then again, perhaps not.

JACQUELINE SAPHRA

The Harmony of the World

Five Readings on Music

Martin Luther
1483–1546

Experience testifies that, after the Word of God, music alone deserves to be celebrated as mistress and queen of the emotions of the human heart (of animals nothing is to be said at present). And by these emotions men are controlled and often swept away as by their lords. A greater praise of music than this we cannot conceive. For if you want to revive the sad, startle the jovial, encourage the despairing, humble the conceited, pacify the raving, mollify the hate-filled — and who is able to enumerate all the lords of the human heart, I mean the emotions of the heart and the urges which incite a man to all virtues and vices? — what can you find that is more efficacious than music?

Martin Luther, *What Luther Says* vol. 2, ed. Ewald M. Plass (Saint Louis, MO: Concordia Publishing House, 1959), 982–983.

Artwork from *The Maastricht Hours*, an early fourteenth-century Christian devotional

Gregory of Nyssa
ca. 335–ca. 395

If the entire world order is a kind of musical harmony whose artisan and creator is God as the Apostle says (Heb. 11:10), then man is a microcosm, an imitator of him who made the world. The divine plan for the world at large sees this image in what is small, for the part is indeed the same as the whole. Similarly, a piece of small, transparent stone reflects like a mirror the entire sun in the same way a small object reflects God's light. Thus I say that in the microcosm, man's nature, all the music of the universe is analogously seen in the whole through the particular inasmuch as the whole is contained by the particular. The structure of our body's organs follows this example, for nature has skillfully constructed it to produce music. Observe the tube-like structure of the windpipe and the harp of the palate where the tongue and mouth resemble a lyre with chord and plectrum.

Since everything natural is compatible with nature, music too is in accord with our human nature. For this reason the great David combined his singing with his teaching on the virtues and sprinkled his lofty teachings with honey's sweetness by which he carefully examines himself and cures our human nature. This cure is a harmonious life which to me the singing suggests through symbols.

Gregory of Nyssa, *Commentary on the Inscriptions of the Psalms*, trans. Casimir McCambley (Hellenic College Press, 2004), 2.

Augustine of Hippo
354–430

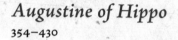

Singers in the harvest, or the vineyard, or at some other arduous toil express their rapture to begin with in songs set to words; then as if bursting with a joy so full that they cannot give vent to it in set syllables, they drop actual words and break into the free melody of jubilation. The *jubilus* is a melody which conveys that the heart is in travail over something it cannot bring forth in words.

And to whom does that jubilation rightly ascend, if not to God the ineffable? Truly is he ineffable whom you cannot tell forth in speech, yet we ought not to remain silent, what else can you do but jubilate? In this way the heart rejoices without words and the boundless expanse of rapture is not circumscribed by syllables.

Augustine, *St. Augustine on the Psalms*, trans. Scholastica Hebgin and Felicitas Corrigan, vol. 2 (Newman Press, 1960), 111–2.

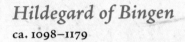

Hildegard of Bingen
ca. 1098–1179

O fiery Spirit, praise to you,
   who on the tympana and lyre
work and play!
   By you the human mind is set ablaze,
the tabernacle of its soul
contains its strength.
   So mounts the will
and grants the soul to taste—
desire is its lamp.
   In sweetest sound the intellect upon you calls,
a dwelling-place prepares for you,
with reason sweating in the golden labor.

Saint Hildegard of Bingen, from "Hymn to the Holy Spirit," trans. Nathaniel
M. Campbell (International Society of Hildegard von Bingen Studies).

Eberhard Arnold
1883–1935

In 1935, Eberhard Arnold spoke to the Bruderhof community about how and how not to sing when gathered for worship.

The misuse of meaningful songs, or even only a lack of understanding and feeling in singing them communally, has a devastating effect. We cannot, for example, sing a deep song after we have just heard of a superficial interpretation of it. The same is true of other songs with a deep meaning. When we sing such songs in real community with the Spirit, we sense something of innermost holiness. Such songs should be sung only at very special moments, only at times of God-given experiences. How can we suggest songs that were once written in the Spirit, with the idea of producing a general feeling that does not exist; how can we sing "God is present with us!" when no one feels that God really is present; how dare we sing "Lord of all, to Thee we bow" when there is no real honoring of God's greatness in the atmosphere of the meeting! This kind of misuse of songs borders on sin against the Holy Spirit.

That is why in our community we often sing apparently superficial songs that only give an inkling of the greatest things – things which at that particular moment should not be brought more strongly to expression. We need an inner criterion, a sensitivity for what is moving the circle at a given moment and for what each song expresses. ➤

Songs of Light: The Bruderhof Songbook (Plough, 1977), xii–xiii.

A DOER'S GUIDE TO

Making Communal Music

In an age of prepackaged tunes, making music with others can feel daunting. We asked seven musicians how to get started.

Violas in Sing Sing

It's never too late to learn an instrument.

NATHAN SCHRAM

Susannah Black: Can you describe yourself and the program?

Nathan Schram: I'm a musician living in Brooklyn where I've been for over twelve years. I have a career as a composer, arranger, and as the violist of the Attacca Quartet, a professional string quartet. Additionally, I am the founder and artistic director of Musicambia, an organization creating music schools in American prisons. Around 2011, I performed at Rikers Island, the main jail complex in New York City. Performing in this isolated place I realized there was a deeper appreciation for music there than in the most elite halls where I have performed around the world. This made me wonder what music could do to combat the growing injustices of America's system of mass incarceration.

The next year I was invited to Venezuela where I studied the music programs they have in prisons, based on El Sistema, an intensive fifty-year-old music-education and antipoverty program. It astounded me how much these prisons were transformed into places of vitality and new beginnings by music.

Deeply inspired upon my return, I created Musicambia. Eight years later we now have programs in seven different facilities around the country. At our flagship program at Sing Sing Correctional Facility we teach everything from music theory and songwriting to individual instrument lessons and ear training. We pride ourselves on helping whatever genres our students envision come to life with their own skill and hard work.

One misconception is that we "bring" music into prisons. However, over the years I have never visited a prison where music wasn't already being made on a daily basis. Our real mission is to advocate for music in prisons and help incarcerated people build a community with their musical peers.

José Antonio Abreu, the founder of El Sistema, called symphonies pictures of perfect societies; sometimes political philosophers use symphonies to illustrate the idea of the common good.

Performances help bring out the very best in people (both inside and outside of prison walls). Working toward a performance, you have a goal. In the rest of society we're often not working for that same performance, so we get stuck in unnecessary conflicts and disagreements. It's one of the many ways that working as a musical ensemble teaches you to be adaptable, focused, and trusting.

Includes free access to *Plough*'s digital version, archives, and

☐ PAYMENT ENCLOSED   ☐ BILL M

Name _____

Address _____

City _____ State _____

Email (for e-newsletter and updates) _____

www.plough.com/subsp

Please allow 4–6 weeks for delivery
of your first issue. For faster service
call **1-800-521-8011** or go to
www.plough.com/subspecial.

BUSINESS REPLY MAIL
FIRST-CLASS MAIL   PERMIT NO. 65   BIG SANDY, TX

POSTAGE WILL BE PAID BY ADDRESSEE

PLOUGH PUBLISHING
PO BOX 8542
BIG SANDY TX 75755-9769

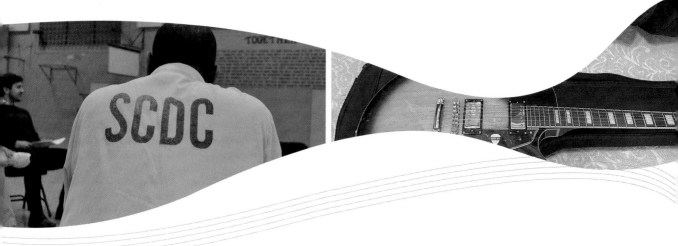

One guy was quoted on your website: "I want to show my wife and kids that I'm starting over with music. I'm a violist now."

In prison, you're defined by the worst thing you've ever done. This constant reminder can keep people from seeing the best in themselves. One reason what we do is so effective is because on day one, we define you as a musician. Instead of that old definition, you're now a violinist. Now, you're a singer. Or maybe you're just a music student. We don't address this directly, but make sure this is reflected in all of our actions as teachers.

We're not "humanizing" the inmates. Everyone is already human there. But we are trying to make the system more humane. I, personally, have been thinking a lot about prison abolition. What could we do instead of locking people up and expecting them to get better? How much better could our society be if we brought out the best in these men and women instead of locking them up for the rest of their lives?

So much of what we do is unspoken. Make the music and the music does its work. We're not going in there trying to make people less angry or nicer to others. I don't know how to do that. But I can show you more about music. And when your focus is music, what's important in life just seems to become a lot clearer.

What are some of your best stories?

There are so many. The first year of Musicambia, this guy came in, not looking us in the eye, and mumbled "Can I practice sax?" I said sure: he didn't get any other chance to play. So he did his thing; I kept teaching. Time went by, and we had a concert: he got up there and played "What a Wonderful World," solo saxophone, in front of two hundred guys. I went up to him, afterwards, to tell him how wonderfully he played. His legs were shaking; all of a sudden he had this light in his eyes, the biggest grin. He said, "That was so exciting. I can't believe I did that." Since that moment, he's been this bright light in the program.

People get that light in their eyes when they're inspired by music. Now he's one of those who brings people together. It was that singular moment that seemed to transform him into someone that could see his immense value in the world.

Everyone wants to belong. Not just those in prison. Everyone. They want to be able to give back, and when they find out how to give, it becomes something that builds them up, as well as everyone around them. ➤

Nathan Schram is founder and artistic director of Musicambia, a nonprofit organization bringing music education and ensemble performance to prisons and jails of the United States. musicambia.org.

Hosting a Hootenanny

The darkness at the edge of a campfire provides a safety zone for even the most self-conscious singer.

ESTHER KEIDERLING

ALMOST EVERYONE HAS SOME SONGS THAT live in their happiest memories. Now cold weather and Covid variants keep us apart, but one day it will be summer again – time for a hootenanny.

My friends Jason and Maureen Swinger host these informal sing-alongs regularly in their backyard, under the stars, around a roaring campfire. Guests arrive with instruments: guitars, banjos, vocal cords. Everyone is welcome, even people who didn't hear about it and just come by to investigate the noise. That's how I stumbled on my first hootenanny in 2015, and I've been coming ever since.

The Swingers use homemade songbooks collected and bound by their neighbor, Tony Potts. His compilation grows as new favorites are suggested; along the way, the Scorpions, Dire Straits, and the Grateful Dead have joined Pete Seeger, Bob Dylan, and Joan Baez. If I don't know a song, I just listen. It doesn't matter if someone sings the tune a bit differently or adds a new verse. We're just a link in the music chain, giving the songs a chance to live on.

To host a hootenanny, you first need songbooks. Annie Patterson and Peter Blood's *Rise Up Singing* is a classic collection, or create your own. Just remember that solo-voice top-ten hits tend to tank fast, no matter how well people know them. Maybe because they're designed to put one person in the spotlight, they seem to sputter out when sung by a group. But band songs from the Beatles to the Eagles to Alabama – now those can fly. (Another tip: In this timeless firelight zone, shared books and flashlights are much more fun than individual phone lyric searches.)

Popular songs work well as starters, but don't neglect folk songs. After all, the sea shanties that were all the rage in 2020 aren't the only muscle-and-blood work songs. There are miners' songs, farming songs, mountain and river music. Songs about winter constellations, piney-wood hills, four strong winds, the streets of London . . . about feeling so broke up, you want to go home. Other voices from other times – men and women who had hard days but made it through.

The campfire, the darkness, and the contagious joy inspire even insecure vocalists to join in. My singing isn't always on key and I don't hit every high note, but that doesn't matter. Folks who shrink from the spotlight may find their voices by firelight, and the lonely or discouraged may find heart as the sparks fly up and someone asks, "Do you know this one?" ➴

Esther Keiderling is a writer who lives at the Fox Hill Bruderhof in Walden, New York.

How to Lullaby

Long before your baby is born, you can start
singing lullabies.

NORANN VOLL

LULLABY. SAY IT TO YOURSELF, SOFTLY,
slowly, repeatedly. It is an old word, formed
sometime during the sixteenth century, whose
onomatopoetic sleepy-time syllables are borne
out in the slumber songs of many lands, in
countless languages and dialects. It is a word
that takes me to my children when they were
small, and before them, back to my earliest
memories of childhood.

My father taught me that a lullaby can be
almost anything provided it is accompanied by
ritual. It takes a special kind of love to get a child
to drift off to accordion music. But my father,
widowed at thirty-nine, achieved this by lighting
a candle each evening in the bedroom I shared
with my sisters, and coaxing folk songs from
his old Hohner until we fell asleep. Some of the
songs he played he learned from his mother – my
grandmother – Gladys Irene Riddell Mason. I
have her to thank for gifting me the unlikely
heart of my own lullaby repertoire: love songs
from the Scottish Hebrides.

Gladys was of Scottish descent and grew up
in Birmingham, England, in the 1920s. Her talent
for singing was recognized early, and her parents
paid for voice lessons. As a young woman,
she worked as a primary school teacher in the
Birmingham slums, announcing breakfast and

leading the ABCs in her resonant alto voice. A
forgotten bus fee was the fortuitous event that
brought my grandparents together. My grandfather Arnold Mason, ever the gentleman, paid
Gladys's fare and so met "the brightest mind,
warmest heart, and bluest eyes in all of England"
(if he said so himself). He soon discovered as
well that his "Glad" also possessed its "sweetest
voice." They married at Christmastime 1933. The
following year Gladys entered and won the
ladies' open competition at the Leamington
Musical Festival. (Ironically for her later trans-
mission of lullabies, it was for her rendition of
Handel's "O sleep, why dost thou leave me?")

Shortly afterward, my grandparents traveled to Germany to visit, and eventually join,
the Bruderhof community. As war swept the
Bruderhof out of its native Germany and on to
adventures in England and the United States by
way of the Paraguayan jungle, my grandmother's
much-loved Hebridean songs took their place in
the community's vast treasure-trove of songs for
all seasons and occasions, gathered and curated
from around the world.

I was twelve years old when I discovered
that I had a gift for singing and that I couldn't
read music. My violin teacher gave up trying
to explain the significance of lines and dots to

my uncomprehending mind and suggested, gently, that I quit. I did, and instead took up voice lessons, with Grandma as my first teacher. "You can learn just fine by ear," Grandma told me as she taught me all the Hebridean love songs she knew. She taught me how to handle high notes, how to enunciate ("If people can't understand the words, there's not much point in the song"), and how to develop control through diaphragmatic breathing.

When I started my own journey as an early childhood educator, Hebridean songs unsurprisingly surfaced as a mainstay among the naptime lullabies I sang to my nursery students. I sang them daily, and in the same order, which the children seemed to love. In my estimation, these are the requirements of any good lullaby: that they gently prepare a child for rest, encourage language development, and strengthen bonds of connection between parent (or caregiver) and child. I had grown up in a home immersed in the songs, old and new, of many lands and cultures, all of which I sang. But invariably, I would return to the haunting, lilting melodies of the windswept Scottish isles.

And then I sang to my own children. Each time I discovered I was pregnant, I began to do two things: keep a baby diary recording the miracle of each day, and sing lullabies to our unborn child. I have three diaries that end abruptly after a few months, and an ache in my heart I have learned to lean into, but I also have lingering and sweet memories of singing to my unborn children who sojourned with us here for a brief time. Lullabies provide an eternal point of loving connection with them.

I have three finished diaries, too, and three grown sons who still know the lullabies I taught them. Perhaps it was merely wish fulfillment on my part, but it seemed to me they recognized, responded to, and claimed as their favorites certain songs from those cold, misty islands – songs I'd sung to them in utero. For as long as possible, I would take turns cradling my children in my arms while I sang through our special order of songs with a reminder that "this one means the next place we're going to fly to is bed." After each child was tucked in, he got his "last song before Mommy has to go." That seemed to help cut down on separation dramas at sleep time.

One of my most precious and enduring memories: my oldest son, still small enough to be snuggled against me, his head on my shoulder and arms around my neck, and his younger brother softly stirring in my womb. I was singing to both children at once, marveling as I watched brotherly bonds form through song. When our third son arrived several years later, the older two would sing each other and their baby brother to sleep when we were away. "Day in the cornfields, I a-reaping, cutting my sheaf and it wasna easy . . . "

The Aboriginal peoples of Australia, where I live now, have storylines and melodies that connect them deep into the past, to their ancestors and their sacred heritage. For me, lullabies do something similar. They bring my children into a circle of song in which they and I are linked to their grandfather and great-grandmother, to a lineage of lullabiers long asleep among the stars, but held close through song. ⤸

Norann Voll lives at the Danthonia Bruderhof in rural Australia with her husband, Chris, and three sons.

Singing Prayers of Resistance

As a radio DJ in Zimbabwe, I learned the power of song to oppose government tyranny and to unite people in prayer.

CHAKA WATCH NGWENYA

MY COUNTRY IS A COUNTRY OF MUSIC. In Zimbabwe, we have songs for every occasion, celebrating, mourning, fighting. But when we need it most, music is a prayer from people who need God, who sing our way back to him because he is always there, no matter how hard it is to see our way forward. The songs go up to him and his strength comes down to us.

In the very hard years of the 1990s and 2000s, I really came to know what these songs of God can mean to oppressed people: it was not safe to speak up, food was hard to come by, and money was not worth the paper it was printed on.

As a radio DJ for Zimbabwe Broadcasting Corporation, I would play gospel music and pray for all those listening in the villages or struggling to keep their households together in the cities. On national radio, you're not allowed to say anything inflammatory or anti-government. So I thought of ways to let the Bible speak. "Do unto others as you would have done to you." "Give justice to the weak and the fatherless."

One day during a very bad time, I just blurted out, "If you are feeling like you cannot go on another day, and you are thinking about ending your life, do not do it. Hold on for one more day. God is there. He knows about you."

I had wondered how many people were listening – I found out! I never got so many letters and calls in my life. They spoke about the songs, and the message of forgiveness I had shared on the three-hour broadcast.

Now my wife and I live in Harlem. We are officers in the Salvation Army, and I co-pastor a small but growing congregation – the Zimbabwe Interdenominational Church.

If you come to our services you will see that song still leads the way to prayer. When a member wants to testify, she begins to hum, then sing. The drum joins in; so does everyone else. Then we hear about a son whose cancer has come back, or a daughter who has lost touch. Or we could be rejoicing; green cards have come through – a family is reunited here in New York City. The song that is chosen tells us first.

My fellow church member Manfred Mukumba likes to say about our songs: "Shona is a strong language. When we sing *Hakuna Wakaita sa Jesu*, it is not enough to translate it as, 'There is no one like Jesus'. It means, 'I have searched everywhere. There is no comparison. Everything else may change, but he will not.'" ➤

Chaka Watch Ngwenya is co-pastor of the Zimbabwe Interdenominational Church in Harlem. He and his wife, Tsitsi, have been Salvation Army officers since 2002. He sings with the gospel band The Soul Seekers.

How to Raise Musical Children

John Feierabend is reviving the insights of the revered music educator
Zoltán Kodály for a new generation.

EILEEN MAENDEL

AS A NEW MUSIC TEACHER AT A PRIVATE
school in England, I received an enthusiastic
welcome: a recital of karaoke recorder "music."
Some students tooted along to a souped-up
backing track, while others were obviously
faking it, each face registering pride and accom-
plishment. I tried not to let my own face show
discouragement at such a loud and unimagina-
tive blast of noise. How could they know that
karaoke is the antithesis of art? Music is so much
more than a mechanical process of playing notes
in the correct sequence. But this was not a time
to be daunted. With time and coaching, the
piercing, prefabricated noise could be turned
into tuneful, beautiful, artful music.

Some years earlier, in Australia, I started
taking courses on the Kodály method. Zoltán
Kodály revolutionized Hungarian schools into
"schools of song" in the 1940s. To Kodály, the
human voice is central to joyous music training,
and the wholesome qualities of his theories,
which draw on social and cultural experiences,
appealed to me at once. As if sampling a
country's best food and literature, teachers
use the richest folk songs and music to show
their students creative, collaborative musical
concepts, aural and written.

My first year of teaching in England was a
learning curve for everyone. For the first few
weeks, every class commenced with the same
routine: one child or another would raise her
hand and ask, "When are we going to play with
the soundtrack again? That music was super
cool." But as time passed, we began to hear and
see a difference. The children listened to each
other, worked and moved together as a group.
They had ideas for folk songs to play, bringing
in crumpled pieces of paper with suggestions.
We worked together to arrange the songs, and
played them on recorders in canons, duets,
and trios. I never heard another request for the
soundtrack. The students owned the music,
and they could hear that the sounds they were
creating were beautiful. That year's Christmas
musical remains a glowing memory for me. Every
rehearsal was like "playing Christmas" – truly
enjoyable for both students and teachers.

The school year continued with an all-school
focus on Italy, to culminate in a party for all the
parents – a celebration of Italian food, song,
music, and dances. There were so many Italian
composers it was hard for the children to choose
which ones we would honor for this festive
occasion. We settled on Vivaldi and Rossini. The
Largo movement of Vivaldi's "Winter" came to life
as we added dynamics and ornamentation. Can
you hear a roomful of students practicing trills?

Then came the thrill of Rossini's *William Tell*

overture. In art class, the children had made silhouettes of their faces in profile. Now, as we played, their parents took turns valiantly wielding bows and arrows and attempting to shoot the apple painted on top of each silhouette. Hilarity ensued. Some silhouettes did not survive. We mostly managed to keep playing through the laughter, and swept to a big finish.

In 2018, I took up a music teaching post in New York, where I had the chance to take a course in Conversational Solfege, a music curriculum for first through eighth grades written and taught by John Feierabend, a leading authority on music and movement development in childhood. Feierabend, who studied under Hungarian Kodály educators, has made Kodály's philosophy accessible to American culture. He passionately believes that music belongs to everyone, though it needs reclaiming from its more recent status as a consumer product.

Luckily this trend is reversible. According to Feierabend, everybody should be able to sing lullabies to their children. Nurturing our babies and toddlers with quality music and finger games helps their physical, emotional, and social development. As the child grows up, age-appropriate activities of moving to classical music, echo songs, and circle games all guide a child to become tuneful, artful, "beat-ful." Clapping games on the playground continue age-old rhymes and traditions. Activities like folk dancing and singing around the campfire reignite the wholesome intergenerational joy of bygone years, when grandparents jiggled babies on their knees, and young people met and fell in love. Why can't it happen again?

It definitely can start at home, but there's also no place like the classroom. My music class begins with pitch exploration games (flying in an airplane, imitating a slide whistle). These are vocal warmups. I follow up with some call-and-response songs like "Down by the Bay." Often these simple tunes teach numeracy, rhyming, or geography. As the children become more confident, they sing in smaller groups until they work up the confidence to solo. We do circle games that have action and movement. Feierabend's curriculum provides directions for dance-like actions to classical music, so rhythm and cadence become a full body experience: while listening to classical music, the children respond with their whole bodies, imagining fast and slow, light and heavy. We build up rhythm skills using body percussion, then add autoharp, tone bells, drums. As one student at a time keeps the beat, I sing a song at their tempo, or recite a poem or nursery rhyme. There's also time for the children to create their own tunes.

I say goodbye to the children by singing them a story, a good classic ballad like "The Tailor and the Mouse," or "Over in the Meadow." Without fail, they say, "Sing it again!" To which I reply, "We'll get to have fun again next week." Better to leave them wanting more.

No class is the same, yet each year the goal is unchanging: that children might be moved by music that sings in their hearts. Many days, I come out of the classroom feeling completely inadequate. Miraculously, the next day the children's inspiration carries the class along, as new songs are composed, new actions born. Music is alive!

Eileen Maendel is a Bruderhof member and lives with her husband at Fox Hill. For more information on the Feierabend technique see feierabendmusic.org.

How to Make Music Accessible

We must build a culture of music-making that welcomes everyone, whether neurodivergent or not.

ADORA WONG

Caitrin Keiper: When and how did you fall in love with music?

Adora Wong: I was one when my four-year-old sister started learning the violin. Apparently, I was enchanted right away and insisted I would play too. I started when I was three and have continued learning ever since!

What were some obstacles you faced along the way? Did your understanding of them change with time?

I was kicked out of a youth orchestra when I was ten because I was "demonstrating anti-social behaviors." Before the first day I'd memorized Beethoven's Fifth Symphony, researched Western orchestral history, and set a goal to one day play *The Nutcracker*. I showed up to the first two rehearsals prepared to play, but during the break I paced around the room to manage my excitement. No one said anything to me about it, so I was surprised when my parents got that phone call. The punishment for stimming [movements that help an autistic person calm down], as I now understand it, was being demoted to a junior strings program where I was with younger kids who could hardly hold their instruments.

There were a few other instances where social misunderstandings got me in trouble. I was embarrassed then, believing it was my

fault. Now I recognize it as being a fault of the system – if a child wants to play an instrument in an orchestra, the focus should be on finding ways for her to be engaged, not about behaviors that are not harming anyone.

What was it like to be diagnosed as autistic after "masking" for many years? How does neurodivergence shape your relationship to music?

I'd known I was "different" since I was a child, so it was a relief when I finally received a diagnosis as an adult. While I am unsure if this connects with autism, I have perfect pitch and auditory-tactile synesthesia, and there is always music running in my mind. Because I'm not a very social person, practicing in isolation for hours at a time doesn't bother me. I also don't experience performance anxiety on stage, and although I wish I didn't have to, I will credit that to years of autistic masking.

What steps can those in the music world take to be more inclusive of other neurodivergent kids?

Many music teachers come strictly from a performance background and have no idea how to interact with children or manage a classroom. This was me as well when I first started teaching,

so I know it is possible to change. At the very minimum, teachers need to understand that all behavior is communication, and be more creative in responding.

You learned English as a fourth (!) language in kindergarten, and have often spoken of growing up with a different perspective than the culture around you.

It's funny because I learned the violin way before I learned English. I started with a Hungarian teacher and musical gestures were our way of understanding each other. Consequently, we found out after more than a year of playing that I couldn't read music at all and was memorizing everything on the spot! I've also seen new immigrant educators teach at a phenomenal level without speaking the same language as the student. This really has me thinking about the way we communicate in music education, and how often "less is more" when it comes to using words to describe musical details.

On the darker side, as an Asian-Canadian violinist, I've had plenty of negative experience with prejudiced thinking in the world of classical music. When I was twenty-one, an Asian professor sat me down and we had the "talk" about how difficult it was going to be for me to make an entrance into orchestral playing as an Asian woman. I've been called the wrong name countless times, even after playing multiple concerts with the same organization. I've had seating arrangements questioned with people wondering if I only made it so far up "to promote diversity." I've had opportunities taken away because I didn't "look" the part for it.

Tell us about your new teaching effort and the project to provide students with violins.

My inspiration comes from the Venezuelan El Sistema program and the centers we already have here in Canada that work toward making music accessible. Classical music lessons can be expensive, and the initial cost of buying an instrument turns many families away. I want every child, regardless of his or her background, to have access to an instrument and quality instruction. I have designed an affordable group class that is geared toward supporting neurodivergent children, but unfortunately this has been put on hold due to the pandemic. However, I am happy to be able to continue teaching private lessons at a reduced cost for families who may require that option.

My dream is to teach in an ensemble that is both accessible and inclusive. By accessible, I mean that there are no financial barriers to joining: it is not overpriced, there is no requirement for expensive private lessons on the side, and there is an instrument bank that students can borrow from. By inclusive, I mean re-evaluating some of our current expectations for orchestral ensembles, and creating a space that is more sensitive to sensory needs. I really think that making classical music more accessible will help solve the other prejudices too because it invites everyone in.

Adora Wong is an early childhood educator in a play-based childcare center working towards a certificate in child development, and a classically trained violinist with a master's degree in music. She lives in British Columbia, Canada.

57

Chanting Psalms in the Dark

In the midst of the Covid pandemic, I became blind.
That's when I discovered the power of chant.

BRITTANY PETRUZZI

Susannah Black: You've had a pretty difficult year, which has led to a pretty wonderful project. Can you tell us about that?

Brittany Petruzzi: Happy to. I've started a YouTube channel; the project is to go through the 150 psalms and record myself chanting them.

I'm calling it the Canticlear Project to reflect the simultaneous clarity and beauty I'm aiming at. The goal is to have a fully recorded chanted psalter that people can listen to and be able to understand every bit of it.

What's the background?

I have a deep love for medieval theology; theater, including musical theater; and the use of language. At the beginning of Covid, I just started thinking that I should do daily psalm-chanting.

Then in December 2020, I found out that I had a brain tumor; less than a week later I was in the hospital getting it removed. It was a seven-centimeter tumor right behind my forehead, squishing my brain back. Enormous amounts of pain. But it was on the meninges, on the outside of my brain. As my neurosurgeon described it, this is the kind of brain tumor you want, if you're going to have a brain tumor.

I'd been having vision problems since April. But the doctors said, once the pressure is relieved, your vision should resolve itself within six months.

But it did not resolve itself. It's been a year, and I am blind.

So I had to reassess my life, to look back on what God has been doing. I was working for a theater company when the pandemic hit; we said, "This is sad, we won't be seeing theater for a while." But it ended up in spring 2021 with me realizing, "Oh, I'm never going to see theater again."

The theater stuff is important because it informs the style of music I'm endeavoring to use. Psalm-chanting is often either beautiful and incomprehensible or a sort of "we're doing the psalms because they are the spinach that God gave us."

But we should find joy in the psalms, and meaning. That's what I'm trying to do: to bring joyful clarity in recording, quality, and expression. And by expression, I mean that the listener should understand both the words and the action behind them.

When I started chanting again, in the hospital, I didn't know very many psalms by memory. But I asked my sister to have my nieces and nephews record a metrical psalm setting and I listened to that.

Chant is different than the kinds of metrical psalms we usually sing in church. Chant uses the natural rhythm of speech. So you take the translation you prefer, and then, guided by the natural rhythm of speech, you break each line up by emphasis, and assign tones to each segment – that's called "pointing" the psalm.

The idea of using the natural rhythm of speech sounds like the way Shakespeare used English speech patterns to make iambic pentameter sound natural.

My training in singing has helped me, but also my familiarity with Shakespeare, my theater training: learning to speak those lines of his for meaning, not just as singsongy poetry.

I'm not against hymns, but it seems to me that if we want to sing in worship to our King, maybe we ought to use the words that he gave us.

Is the project helping you in your transition to being a blind Bible-reader?

It's planting the words of scripture in my heart. I started with Psalm 121, because when I could see, I was big on trail-running, and often when I was running full speed down steep hills, Psalm 121 would pop into my head: "He will not allow your foot to stumble."

When I was diagnosed, that's the one I thought of. I used it to calm down my pagan friends who were freaking out.

I would say, "Look, the Lord has had me for thirty-three years, and he still has me now; don't worry about it." They were like, "Okay, I guess." It's been – I keep wanting to say an eye-opening – experience to realize that the faith I had my entire life, when it comes down to it, is real. I believe all this. I was resting in the Lord. My hope is partly that when others listen to this project, they'll also have the psalms running through their heads, to have those words to lean on, to help them begin to rest too.

The truth is that this has been a blessing. People like to throw around phrases like "God has a plan for you." All those vague moralistic, therapeutic, deistic phrases become true in light of the deeper reality of God's providence, his purpose. You're forced to say, "How can I work with God rather than just suffer and get bitter under this hard providence?"

And one way to work with him is, precisely, to pray. One idea that C. S. Lewis explores is that when we pray we are fellow workers with God, working on his big project of building the kingdom.

Chanting psalms would be, in that context, something that literally advances the plot of God's work in his world, which is also our work.

What I'm doing is fighting. My hope is that YouTube high command doesn't cotton on to how political this is, that chanting psalms is one of the things that brings down God's enemies. 🔖

Brittany Petruzzi is a freelance theater artist. She lives in Kernersville, North Carolina.

...ssed for all of my adult life. I am closer to 60 than I am 50. ...n were alive, so that I could walk with him....to tell him the...
...n every last second of every breath.

REPLY

8 replies

...ke you find it easy"

...eally resonates with me. As a person with social anxiety issues, I al... ...have so many friends and be so carefree with each other. It's neve... ...be nice for them.

REPLY

...plies

...n (edited)

...tly took his life, i didnt play this song in hi... He walked away in silence for the last 7... ...is presence, i raised him... ...sing, i wasnt left a letter...

> yesterday I taught the Song of Songs & we discussed the line "love is strong as death." I quoted Sonnet 147: "Desire is death." a student chimed in: "Love is a battlefield." gen x casts a long shadow.
>
> —*Michael Robbins, on Twitter*

> Has it ever struck you that life is all memory, except for the one present moment that goes by you so quick you hardly catch it going? —Tennessee Williams
>
> —*Quoted by Sameoldfitup 2008 in the YouTube comments to the video for Squeeze's "Another Nail in My Heart"*

Reading the Comments

Fans of 1980s post-punk and new wave find community and catharsis online.

PHIL CHRISTMAN

EARLY IN 2021, I found that my emotions were becoming a burden to me. What was strange about my predicament was that most days I also felt disturbed by my *lack* of emotion, or the puniness of what I did feel: peevishness where there ought to be grief, a washed-out melancholy that hardly rose to the level of mourning. I felt bad, and I felt – *pace* the grammarians – bad*ly*. My lukewarm misery hardly seemed worthy of its causes. (To name a few: my father's health collapsed; my wife's father died; a friend's beloved child went in and out of hospitals; a

friend died; our cat died; the planet's warming; Bernie lost.) This feeling alternated with nightly spikes of intense anxiety. My chest felt too tight for air to pass through, and I watched, for hours, the stupidest TV shows I could find, hoping to distract my brain from its own churning – a churning that went on regardless of the content I fed it – that would, if I strove to think about nothing, churn *about itself.*

The best artistic evocation of that churning I've ever heard is Joy Division's 1979 classic "She's Lost Control," with its simple drum pattern and ascending guitar figure that repeat

---

Phil Christman teaches at the University of Michigan and is editor of the Michigan Review of Prisoner Creative Writing. *He is the author of the new essay collection* How to Be Normal *(Belt, 2022).*

themselves in a tighter and tighter spiral until the song mercifully fades out. The song is meant to evoke an epileptic attack, of the sort that its singer Ian Curtis suffered with increasing frequency in the months before his May 1980 suicide. As for what grief ought to feel like, the scale of the sadness that I longed for but couldn't achieve, that, too, had been perfectly expressed by the same band, in 1980's "Atmosphere," with its slow pace and its echo-heavy production (courtesy of Martin Hannett, who also died young), the contrast between Stephen Morris's cavernous drums and Bernard Sumner's high, pretty, icy synth figures. Listening to it is like walking through a darkened cathedral. Curtis's otherworldly, somehow-already-posthumous vocals and Peter Hook's luminous bass lead you through.

So it hardly seems accidental that I reached for these songs in my distress. Joy Division are a known favorite among the mentally disturbed, and in any case, we tend, in depressing times, to revert to the music that we listened to in our youth, which for me is post-punk and new wave. But the fact that I found myself, one evening, not only playing and replaying old Joy Division clips on YouTube, but *reading the comments* on those clips – that I must chalk up to the positively humiliating effects of pandemic loneliness. To read the comments on anything on the internet – an article, a video, a photo of an unimpeachably cute dog – is usually a bullet train to despair. But that evening, I discovered that people who comment on Joy Division videos are delightful, responding to the impersonal intimacy of the music with an equally disarming, if less artful, vulnerability. One commenter describes the band as his "mental backup" during the

years when he was "getting abused by a family 'friend.'" Another person details the strange connection between the band and his father, who "always had problems in his life" because "he was a child that wasn't planned."

I once heard of a program in which prisoners read Shakespeare and then, rather than mounting full performances, discuss the texts, reading them aloud, repeating the lines to themselves and to each other. Are these the right words, at last? Have I found the speech that will explain me to myself? Commenters on "Atmosphere" do a similar exercise with that song's chillingly equivocal refrain "Walk / in silence / Don't walk away / In silence," and with the devastating line that opens its first verse, "people like you find it easy," a line all the more powerful because Curtis doesn't specify who finds what easy. It's a bitten-off accusation, one he's too overwhelmed to finish making. A commenter named OMEN writes, for example:

> My brother just recently took his life, i didn't play this song in his funeral because its a secret Ode i play in my mind for him . . . He walked away in silence for the last 7 years of his life . . .

A commenter posting under the name Nathan Parsons says: "As a lifelong sufferer of depression that 'people like you find it easy' line has always struck a chord." TheMusicalElitist – speaking for so many of us musical elitists – writes, "As an Autistic person, this is what autism feels like: the feeling of isolation from the rest of the world who find it so easy to communicate. I will always walk away in silence."

OMEN's post is not the only one to reference a beloved person's funeral. One woman writes that her ex-partner had wanted

"Atmosphere" played at his funeral; when he died, she tried to honor his wishes but was overruled by the family. "sorry ronnie it was out of my control," she wrote. "I play this and think of you."

The reader can explain easily enough what was going on with me that day. I felt for the dead-too-young Ian Curtis – a brilliant artist and flawed man, a Tory domestic abuser and a part-time social-service provider noted for his compassion – what I didn't know how to feel for the people around me. It's safe to mourn a dead rock star; it hurts to mourn a friend. Like most explanations of emotional life, this one sounds both logical and somehow disconnected from the experience it's supposed to explain, in the same way that I don't know how to connect my mild despair or sharp anxiety to their ostensible causes. When people make logic out of my emotions for me, it feels like they're constructing mottes and baileys. My instinctive response might be summarized: *People like you find it easy.*

If I was displacing my personal sadnesses onto Ian Curtis, I wasn't alone there, either. Every year, on the anniversary of his death, another wave of comments came: RIP Ian, and thank you. Someone posting under the name Daniel Day wrote, "Clinically depressed for all of my adult life. [. . .] I wish Ian were alive, so that I could walk with him . . . to tell him that overcoming the urge is worth every last second of every breath." Maybe he's reassuring himself, but the anonymous charity of his comment, placed where any number of young or middle-aged depressives might stumble across it, reassures me as well.

THUS I BECAME an informal student of the YouTube comment threads on the punk and post-punk bands of the 1970s and 1980s, just as, in adolescence, I had been an informal student of the bands themselves. Born in 1978, I came to this music already a bit late, and I often felt isolated in finding the era artistically fertile as well as amusingly camp. Joy Division and its successor band New Order nicely symbolize the various forms of that fertility. They began as a punk band called Warsaw, making amateurish and – to the extent the listener deciphers the lyrics – aimlessly provocative music. (All three band names are, in keeping with the punk-rock ethos, a calculated attempt to offend the generation that lived through World War II, also known as Mum and Dad.) But bassist Peter Hook couldn't hear himself over the racket Warsaw generated, so he played higher on the neck than usual, generating an unusual timbre. Such lucky accidents – the luckiest their encounter with Hannett, who among other things rigorously separated the instruments, creating a sense of sonic detachment and isolation that matched Curtis's lyrics, and

introduced a slight digital delay that makes the songs seem to echo themselves, like Beckett's Krapp speaking over his old tapes – transformed a sound that was all outward force into one that was all inward reflection. After Curtis's suicide, as New Order, the remaining members further investigated the power of machines, and now it was the contrast between the mechanical perfection of the synths, the high, awkward voice of Bernard Sumner, and the warmth of Hook's bass that created dramatic tension. They started by leveraging the expressive power of amateurism; they continued by embracing an analytic coldness; and then, with the help of machines, they became unlikely, Warholian global pop stars playing catchy dance music. That is new wave in a nutshell.

Well, almost. You also have to factor in history. The kids who listened to what was first punk, then post-punk, then new wave, then the hopelessly vague "alternative rock" came to maturity at roughly the moment the promises of New Deal America and Family Britain – that you would outdo your parents with the help of

the state – were dropped. They were shadowed by the memory of two spectacular but failed revolutionary moments closely associated with pop music: the hippies and the punks. These alterna-teens thus fetishized outcasts and rebels, but the examples nearest to hand were failed rebels. Even the terms used to discuss the music reflect a sense of failure: "Postpunk," like "postmodern," does not describe anything; it only records one's helpless subjection to time – punk happened, and then another thing happened, because things have a way of happening. "New wave," a euphemism coined by a record-company head who didn't like the word "punk," is even worse: wave after wave after wave, and they all crash. The gloriously singable refrain of the Sex Pistols' greatest song was "no future," and yet the future kept coming. New wave relates to punk as the compromises that enable us to live relate to the dream of impossible perfection. This is why even lesser new wave is aesthetically interesting: it is melancholy. It is the thing you do after the thing that was supposed to end everything.

T HE ODD LITTLE non-community that I found within the comments sections of other bands' videos, too, was shadowed by failure, by the capitulations that constitute adulthood. Responding to the joyous "Our Lips Are Sealed," by the Go-Go's, which features the band illegally cavorting in a fountain, a commenter makes the immortal complaint of age to youth:

> 47 now and watching this makes me cry. Such happy carefree times. Life will never be like that again. This brought me right back to those wonderful 80s when music

was great and everyone wasn't tied to a phone and social media.

Surely this records a disappointment that runs far deeper than Twitter.

A comment on Bananarama's "Cruel Summer" sounds like a German Romantic who has been rather flatly translated:

> This song brings a kind of a sad, nostalgic longing of a magical time long gone . . . it is almost as if I want to relive it, but at the same time reminds me of the pain of something that can not be anymore [. . .] now it's just a long cruel summer.

Say it to yourself in a Werner Herzog voice.

But the passage of time brings joy as well as loss. I found myself especially moved to read, under David Bowie's melancholy 1980 video for "Ashes to Ashes": "It feels really good to hear this song and be 5 years clean from heroin." (The comment is attributed to one Buzz Lightyear.) People share their joys in these spaces as well as their sorrows. Under Modern English's luminous Cold War love song "I Melt With You," you can find story after story like this one, from a fellow who calls himself Cliff Cardinal:

> I had a girlfriend since may 1981. This song i sang to her in 1983. That was 37 yrs ago. I was so in love with her, she was 14 and i was 16 when we met at an arcade in Santa Cruz at the boardwalk, 39 yrs ago. We got married in may 1986, had 4 sons and 1 daughter. We now have 10 grandchildren. Every time i play this song it just makes me melt and remember the time i had a girlfriend that was just drop dead gorgeous. She is still so beautiful.

The "melting" Cliff describes here isn't what Modern English had in mind – the song is about experiencing nuclear apocalypse with your best girl by your side, or even closer – but it *is* the sort of melting I felt when I read his note.

WHO KNOWS WHETHER it is ultimately pain or joy that stabs deepest, anyway? One evening, tired of being sad, I cued up what I thought was a safely cheerful, anthemic song, Big Country's "In a Big Country." Here is what I read immediately under it:

> I was incarcerated in a state prison outside of Harrisburg, Pennsylvania. The local rock station played this song often. Always made me feel better. I am a free man now and appreciate this song so much more knowing where I came from.

A heavy joy, this comment, but a joy. What was even more heartening was the speed with which several other commenters affirmed this man's good vibe. "Ah hope your life is good. Music can save your life it has mine and comedy x," wrote Marian. She went on: "The internet can be such an impersonal place and I often wonder and hope for the people you see comment." Me too, Marian.

Witnessing this exchange got me as close to weepy as I get. It was too much. So I went back up to the search box and typed in the happiest song I know – the ecstatic B-52s paean to no-frills two-person global travel, "Roam" – and, reader, I swear to you that this is what my eyes landed on: "Song came out when I was in my 20's, they just offered me early retirement today, time to Roam." I hope that this poster, for whom I choked back a sob, is on a sunlit boat, watching what's left of the whales.

I also hope she's a real person. On the internet, you can't be sure, and I've definitely read my share of what sounded like bots, or pranks, or malicious fictions. I felt a little twinge of doubt when a poster whose name appeared in Cyrillic characters shared the following information in response to Tears For Fears's "Pale Shelter": "I'm dying of lung cancer. Only this music comforts me." "Pale Shelter" slaps, but really – *no* other music? Not even other Tears For Fears songs? At any rate, if this commenter is real, I apologize. But I will not apologize for doubting the very first response to him, her, or them: "Do not die!! There is a cure for you!! You can use soursop leaf tea!!!"

And in a year when multiple police departments have been caught committing social-media fabrication to counter protests, am I to believe that the following, which I found underneath Billy Idol's greatest moment as a solo performer, really happened?

> I was with my friend once at HyVee waiting in the long buffet line with a bottle of wine and dessert, waiting to order some sushi and chow mein to take home and they started played this song. Of course, we start singing along [. . .] Right as we were getting into it, I saw two cops standing behind us also singing along and bobbing their heads. One of them winked at me and the other one chuckled and suddenly they started singing louder with us and it ended up being an awesome short-lived karaoke party.

They go on to buy the cops dinner. "Despite everything that's been going on in the world," the commenter concludes, "it's nice to have moments like these." Now, maybe this happened! On the other hand, maybe there's a police union's intern somewhere who needs to let us Billy Idol fans dance with ourselves in peace.

These are the sorts of limits that online goodwill always runs up against. Art, and our sincere, artless responses to it, can evoke heart and soul – I was going to cheekily reference T'Pau's 1987 hit "Heart and Soul" here, till I found that the coward who manages the band's YouTube page has disabled comments – but we need flesh-and-blood presence too. The sages of the comment section acknowledge as much. The other day I listened to "Atmosphere" again, and noticed a comment I hadn't seen before. Reflecting on Ian Curtis's suicide, a fan wrote, with that mixture of kindness and acidity that the Brits have spent centuries perfecting: "Please talk to your wanker neighbour. They may be boring, but I prefer to speak to them than never have the opportunity." That's a truth. Who is my neighbor, though? During a rotten year, these strangers helped at least one remote neighbor feel less alone. ⮜

The Tapestry of Sound

Hildegard of Bingen meets Yuri Gagarin in the music of a Grammy Award-winning composer.

CHRISTOPHER TIN

Based in Los Angeles, Christopher Tin is a composer of music for the concert hall and for film and video game soundtracks. His song "Baba Yetu," a setting of the Lord's Prayer in Swahili, was the first piece of music written for a video game to win a Grammy Award. Plough's Joy Clarkson spoke with him about themes that bind many cultures together: the fear of death, the need for rebirth, and the desire to fly.

Joy Clarkson: Your music is very international. You draw on many source texts and write in many languages. How did this love of cultures and languages become central to your music?

Christopher Tin: I've seen a lot of the world. I was very lucky in that my parents love to travel and they trotted me along with them every-where. I've met a lot of people, tasted a lot of different cuisines, and heard a lot of languages over the years. My music comes from a basic love of experiencing and seeing the world. But there's also a love of history.

At university and as a postgraduate, I majored in English and music. I was very interested in the history of ideas, the history of thought, aesthetic trends, intellectual and philosophical trends, how they feed into each

Sim Chan, *TwinklingCity no. 6*, oil on canvas, 2017

other, and how every generation of artists and philosophers builds upon the work that their predecessors laid down. I get excited by things like that. I get excited by the interconnectedness of people and cultures and traditions across the world, but also the interconnectedness of ideas through the centuries. I just find that really interesting, and I write about what brings me joy. And that tends to be historical and cultural things.

My first album, *Calling All Dawns,* contains twelve songs in twelve different languages. It is all about life, death, and rebirth. The source texts pull on everything from ancient myths, to prayers, to some original texts. The album weaves all these together to create a story, a monomyth as Joseph Campbell would call it. It's a monomyth about how we are all connected by a common human experience that sort of winds through each of our lives like a thread. Taken together, all of our experiences around the world form this elaborate tapestry of humanity.

The theme of tapestry seems like a key concept in your music. Is that true?

Totally. Even the way that I write my orchestral parts and my choral parts relates to this idea, this synecdoche, of a tapestry. I very much think of an orchestra as a series of individuals who play one note at a time. And yes, there are instruments that will play chords, multiple notes at a time, but I tend to think of everyone as a thread. And when I compose my pieces, these threads move in parallel, they move in counterpoint, they intertwine, they spread out, they come together, they split, they join, they do all these different things. To me, a piece of music is a bunch of moving horizontal

threads that just kind of fly around in the air and tie themselves together. That's how I think of music. I don't think of it vertically; it is the horizontal motion of individual voices or instruments moving through time, being aware of each other, connecting with each other, and all moving toward the big finale.

A really good example of this musically is your album *To Shiver the Sky*, which intricately interweaves themes, motifs, and voices. That album is ambitious: an eleven-movement oratorio about the history of mankind's quest to conquer the heavens, a history of aviation told through music. In doing that, you draw on the words of significant figures throughout history. Why did you start that album with a text from Hildegard of Bingen?

I chose Hildegard of Bingen because I wanted to establish the narrative arc of *To Shiver the Sky.* It's all about achieving flight, and being up amongst the sky and the clouds and the stars. Long before we were actually able to achieve flight, the concept of being closer to God meant that we did things like build giant cathedrals. The spires went higher and higher, so that we could reach upward toward God. And this was a sentiment to which I wanted to allude early on in the album. Our desire to fly is not just an engineering thing. It's also for religious reasons. We want to be elevated. We want to be close to God.

Hildegard obviously has a lot of writings, but she's a composer herself as well. I wanted to write something that sounded like something that she would've written, which is why her song is constructed as a plainchant. But I wanted to dress it up with twenty-first century orchestrations and inject it with my own

personal style. Because all of this needs to be pulled together under one sonic umbrella and that umbrella is my personal aesthetic taste. So Hildegard's movement really kicks off the journey, but I also bring Hildegard's theme back at the very end of the album. We end with a one-two punch: Yuri Gagarin's first words when he returned from being the first man in outer space, followed by John F. Kennedy's, "We choose to go to the moon." The "We Choose to Go to the Moon" movement kicks off with the same melodic line as the Hildegard of Bingen movement, because everything needs to be sort of bookended, in my mind. And the way you do that in music is you transplant motifs from one piece to the other.

We might assume in our modern world that the moon landing was primarily an achievement of technology, but by tying Hildegard's theme in with JFK's you remind us that the desire to fly is reflective of a more universal desire, present not just in different cultures, but throughout time: the desire to transcend ourselves, touch the sky, to be close to God.

Yes, they're hundreds of years apart, but the basic human impulse is the same. A lot of my music focuses on this notion of synecdoche: the part reflecting the whole. I like to zero in on a piece and have it be a microcosm of the rest of the album. One example of this is my Japanese song, which is track two on *Calling All Dawns*, "Mado Kara Mieru." In itself it is a miniature cycle embedded into this much larger cycle. And that piece itself is built around this idea of seasons, which is obviously a cyclical sort of thing.

It's like a Russian doll! It reminds me: Hildegard talks about microcosms and macrocosms. She thinks of human beings as microcosms of the universe. If we want to understand the universe, we look to human beings. And when we look to human beings, we understand something about the universe. To understand the infinite, we look to the finite.

That is, in essence, the title of my second album, *The Drop That Contained the Sea.* What you just said mirrors, almost perfectly, the Sufi concept that, just like every single drop of water contains the essence of the entire ocean, each individual contains the essence of all humanity. And here we have another example where these parallel thoughts are independently arrived at by a German mystic in the twelfth century and Sufi philosophers.

I think that's the brilliant thing about music in a way. It shortcuts a lot of these cerebral processes that we all have and just gets you to the good vibes, without really having to work it out in your mind, like, "Why does this delight me?" Oh, it's not just because this motif recurs in movements four and eleven or whatever. It just does. And you get the joy out of it. ⤳

Christopher Tin, 2015

Interview conducted on November 22, 2021

In the Aztec Flower Paradise

*For the ancient Nahua poets, the way to the holy
runs through beauty.*

JOSEPH JULIÁN GONZÁLEZ

and MONIQUE GONZÁLEZ

Isabel Santos,
*Mythological
Owls* (detail),
acrylic paint
on bark paper,
2020

O N A CRISP FALL MORNING sometime in the early 1990s, driving down the I-5 from Los Angeles to California's Central Valley, I began to hear a piece of music in my mind. As a composer this wasn't an unusual experience for me, and I enjoyed the interloping melody as a background track to a leisurely drive. As the miles flew past I began noticing details: a choir, a full symphony orchestra, and Aztec percussion. In fascination I began to wonder who had written it . . . Carlos Chávez? Silvestre Revueltas? Another Mexican composer? It sounded like a concert Mass; I heard the words of the *Kyrie* mixed with Aztec rhythms and instrumentation. Composer after composer passed through my mind before it dawned on me that what I was hearing was completely new; it was being "composed" as I heard it.

Joseph Julián González is a composer for television, film, and live orchestra performances. He and his wife, Monique González, are working on a book on the role of Aztec flower poetry in the conversion of Mexico.

Any artist would kill for this type of inspiration. In excitement, I unconsciously pushed down the accelerator and was quickly rewarded with the strobing lights of the California Highway Patrol in my rearview mirror. After pulling to the side of the road, I scrambled for a piece of paper to notate the music I had been hearing in my mind. A few minutes later – with a speeding ticket in hand – I proceeded more slowly down the rest of the grade, mentally mapping out the concert Mass I would spend the next several years composing: *Misa Azteca*. Since then, the piece has been performed worldwide, from the Vatican to the Sydney Opera House. But all these years later, I'm still pondering the beauty and mystery I found in what became my source text: Aztec poetry.

The *tlamatinime* believed there was a connection between beauty and the divine, and used the symbol of the flower to open the portal between them.

From the beginning of *Misa Azteca*'s composition, I was inspired by Benjamin Britten's 1962 *War Requiem*, which combines Wilfred Owen's Great War poetry with the text of the Latin Mass for the Dead. I decided to mingle Aztec poetry with the Mass text in order to explore the religious sentiments present in both cultures, and to tell a story of the spiritual and religious transformation that occurred in Mexico, and for that matter most of the Americas. The Aztecs were one of over fifty Indigenous peoples – collectively known as the Nahua, speakers of Nahuatl – that lived in the Valley of Mexico at the time of the conquest. (I use "Aztec" and "Nahua" interchangeably to talk about the people who have lived in this area for well over a thousand years). An important aspect of Nahua culture was their unique compilation of orally transmitted song poems. The anthropologist John Bierhorst translated a large body of this classic Nahuatl literature in his 1985 English book *Cantares Mexicanos:*

Songs of the Aztecs. Of the song poems collected by Franciscan friars, this collection contains just under a hundred. The texts, which include both pre- and post-conquest song poetry, were collected from the lips of Indigenous elders from 1558 to 1561, just four decades after the fall of Mexico at the hands of Hernán Cortés.

In the pages of the *Cantares Mexicanos* I sought texts that mirrored each movement of the Mass. It was not difficult to find Aztec equivalents to match most of the themes: the Kyrie ("Lord, Have Mercy") is about asking for forgiveness of sin, while the Gloria ("Glory to God in the Highest") is about worship. I easily incorporated poems on these themes into the composition. However, when I started to compose the Sanctus ("Holy, Holy, Holy is the Lord God Sabaoth") and began looking for texts that captured the theme of holiness, another world opened up to me.

In Nahua philosophy and poetry, holiness is an actual place – a flower world paradise. We get a glimpse of this other realm through flowers, which serve as symbols of earthly beauty that gesture to divine reality. Flowers, in their beauty, emanate the holy, and singing – especially about flowers! – was the most important artistic expression of that holiness in the Nahua world view. But Nahua poetry is not easy to understand. The Franciscans were so baffled by these obscure and esoteric song poems that they considered them untranslatable. The Mexican anthropologist and historian Miguel León-Portilla addressed this aporia in *Aztec Thought and Culture* (1967), arguing that the people of pre-conquest Mesoamerica expressed their philosophical considerations in a highly specific metaphorical and poetic style. This melding, a genre called *in xochitl in cuicatl*, "flower and song," along with the Nahuatl language itself, expresses Nahua philosophy. In fact, the word *nahuatl* means "clarity" and describes an entire culture dedicated to philosophical clarity and truth.

For millennia, Indigenous Nahua sages called the *tlamatinime*, or learned ones, composed song poems about the nature of truth and reality. They dictated them to the *tlacuiloque*, highly skilled artists who preserved the poems in pictorial writings that served as mnemonic devices helping *tlamatinime* to memorize and sing their poems to kings and in public rituals. As León-Portilla puts it:

> The wise men did not believe that they could form rational images of what is beyond, but they were convinced that through metaphors, by means of poetry, truth was attainable. . . . Only through metaphor and poetry could they utter some truth about, and thus communicate with, the divine.

The *tlamatinime* believed there was a connection between beauty and the divine, and used the symbol of the flower to open the portal between them. Flowers and songs, therefore, can hardly be distinguished:

> My flowers shall not cease
>   to live;
> my songs shall never end;
> I, a singer, intone them;
> they become scattered, they are
>   spread about.

Through flower-song the wise men asked the hard questions about life and existence: How do we know what is real? Is life just a dream? What is the purpose of life? What is truth? Can you find it on earth? One flower poet writes:

> Is there perchance any truth to
>   our words here?
> All seems so like a dream, only do we rise
>   from sleep,
> Only on earth do our words remain.

Isabel Santos, *Aztec Eagles Nest*, acrylic paint on bark paper, 2021

About the artist: Isabel Santos is an Indigenous Mexican from the state of Guerrero. Her mother tongue is Nahuatl, the native language of the Aztecs. The tradition of making bark paper and using it for documents and artwork has been kept alive since the Aztec era. Santos grew up in a household of artisans, and her mother and grandmother were also bark paper artists.

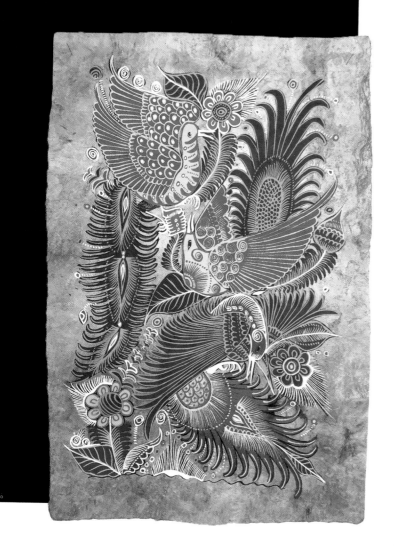

a four-petaled flower. Archaeologists, anthropologists, and linguists observe that this flower world, as a solar, spiritual, and religious theme, is prevalent not only throughout Mesoamerica but also across the American Southwest. The ever-present image of the four-petaled flower along with the song poems of the *tlamatinime* demonstrate a belief in the transcendental aspects of beauty.

The Nahua notion of the flower world paradise resonates strikingly with the Platonic idea of the forms: that there is some ideal of perfection that we have in our minds and hearts. For instance, we possess an image of a perfect flower in our minds and with that we can judge which of two roses is more beautiful. In this way, earthly beauty triggers a remembrance or sense of divine beauty. Pope emeritus Benedict XVI describes this "remembrance" of the divine as a process of transcendental participation, humanity's propensity for moving towards transcendence, a "godlike constitution of our being" oriented away from

Nahua philosophy holds that truth, like beauty, must be transcendent and eternal, and flowers became metaphorically representative of both – the divine plane where truth can be found is the flower world paradise. This notion originates with the mother culture of Mesoamerica, the Olmec, whose art notably features a recurring motif of four points surrounding a central element – the four cardinal directions intersecting a central axis that reaches vertically to heaven, otherwise known as the *axis mundi*. Its intersecting planes connect, imaginatively and in three dimensions, the worldly and the eternal. In Mesoamerica, the conjunction of the *axis mundi* often manifests itself as

ourselves. Beauty, like truth, is a metaphysical, transcendental reality; our experience of it can lift us from the material world to an encounter with being itself, or the ultimate source of beauty: God. Benedict agrees with both Plato and Saint Augustine that an encounter with beauty takes us to that transcendental realm. Beauty is, as Pope John Paul II described it in his encyclical, the *veritatis splendor*, the splendor of truth.

The Mesoamerican idea of holiness sees flowers as just such a point of contact with the divine, and the *tlamatinime* were preoccupied with the search for truth *through – via –* beauty. The first song poem in *Cantares Mexicanos,* the

Cuicapeuhcayotl, whose title could be translated as either the "Beginning of the Songs" or "The Origin of the Songs," is preeminent among them. It summarizes man's quest for truth, albeit in a uniquely Mesoamerican manner. Here is the first verse:

I ponder within my heart, where will I gather the holy, fragrant flowers?
Who will I ask?
I truly desire to ask the honorable golden hummingbird, the honorable jade hummingbird, I wish to ask the troupial butterfly.
Truly, they know where blossom the holy fragrant flowers:
I wander here through the forest of trogon birds,
I truly desire to wander through the forest of roseate swans and flowers
There they may be gathered, with dew glowing with sunlight,
There they blossom.
Perhaps I will see them there?
If they showed them to me, I will fill my *tilma* and with them I will greet the nobles, with them I will make the lords happy.

It cannot be a coincidence that the event which ultimately converted the Americas to Christianity involved roses and a *tilma*: the story of Saint Juan Diego and the apparition at Tepeyac Hill in 1531. In this Marian apparition, which many credit with the conversion of Mexico, not only did the Lady of Guadalupe appear to Juan Diego and speak in his Nahuatl tongue, she offered a sign of her blessing: roses, unlike any Juan Diego had ever seen, growing miraculously. Just as in the Nahua poem above, the Virgin Mary filled Juan Diego's *tilma* – his cloak – with roses, leaving with them a miraculous imprint of her image. Though this apparition would transform Mexican culture, it preserved and embraced as true what the *tlamatinime* had long perceived in their poetry: holiness can be revealed through flowers, truth found through beauty.

The Nahua sought the ultimate source of truth through beauty, and in my own life, so have I. One day in 2008 I found myself walking up the steps of the church near my house. Within its walls, gorgeous strains of ancient motets and chants rang out, beckoning me to return to the church of my fathers. A nearly forgotten form of the Mass drew me back to faith, with musical beauty and a rhythm of prayer and longing that echoes back across the centuries. In the same way the Nahua were drawn to God through the magnificence of their ancient flower poetry, I was brought back to God through the splendor of the Tridentine Latin Mass, which has remained relatively unchanged for over centuries; ancient beauty gesturing beyond itself.

It is in the bosom of this tradition that I have begun to resolve the deeper questions that arose as I wrote my *Misa Azteca*, and sought the theme of holiness in Nahua poetry. For what is the Sanctus but a never-ending song praising the source of infinite beauty and truth? As the ancient poets sing:

Certainly, it is elsewhere in the hereafter where there is true joy . . .
Truly there is another life in the hereafter.
I wish to go there, I wish to sing amongst the multitude of precious birds.
I wish to enjoy the holy flowers.
The fragrant flowers, the ones that please the heart
Only their intoxicating fragrance makes one happy, their fragrance intoxicates. ➴

> It cannot be a coincidence that the event which ultimately converted the Americas to Christianity involved roses.

BENJAMIN CROSBY

Is Congregational Singing Dead?

It's time to make church music weird again.

Thomas Webster,
The Village Choir,
oil on panel, 1847

IT IS EASY TO ASSUME that congregational singing has always been a part of Christian worship. Indeed, if anything it has something of an old-fashioned air at present, conjuring up seemingly timeless images of dusty, yellowed hymnals, of the old mainline church in the center of town, of Garrison Keillor paeans to the Lutherans of Lake Wobegon. But of course, none of those images are in fact timeless, and congregational song has a quite precise history: like the hymnal, the mainline churches, and Lutherans, congregational singing is a product of the Protestant Reformation.

Today, however, the practice of congregational singing in church is threatened by a sea change in how people relate to music outside of church. All is not lost, however: the church, if it commits to the weirdness of congregational singing, might work to rebuild a culture of communal music-making within and outside the church, use that culture to invite people into the church, and – most importantly – continue to offer psalms, hymns, and spiritual songs to Almighty God.

Of course, it is not that music was wholly absent from Christian worship before Martin Luther nailed his theses to the Wittenberg church door. In the Christian West prior to the Reformation, the priest would have chanted the Mass, and in larger parishes and cathedrals a choir might have sung the principal parts. In their monasteries and convents, monks and nuns marked the hours of prayer by chanting services of great complexity. But music in worship was generally the preserve of clergy, monastics, and professionals. It was a great innovation of the Reformers in both Lutheran and Calvinist churches to open up participation in music during worship to all Christians. And what a transformation of the experience of public Christian worship this must have been! The Lutherans were the first great hymn writers, with Luther himself composing numerous hymns still in use by Christians of all traditions today (one can even find "A Mighty Fortress Is Our God" in Roman Catholic hymnals). The Reformed typically restricted church music to metrical psalmody, that is, verse paraphrases of psalms. Many of the psalm-tunes that early Reformed composers wrote are also still in use today, even as most contemporary Reformed churches allow a somewhat wider array of music in worship.

Not only was congregational singing a Protestant development, but it was also a significant means of Protestant success, of building popular attachment to the new articulations of doctrine,

---

Benjamin Crosby is a priest in the Episcopal Church serving in the Anglican Church of Canada and a doctoral student in ecclesiastical history at McGill University.

new ways of worship, and new churches that emerged from the convulsions of the sixteenth century. Andrew Pettegree, in his excellent *Reformation and the Culture of Persuasion* (2005), notes the incredible popularity of both hymns and metrical psalmody, in church and beyond. Protestants sang these new songs at worship, at home, at work; such music became an important badge of Protestant identity. Indeed, in a darker key, violent iconoclasm and Protestant-Catholic street fighting were often carried out to the sound of the new Protestant music. The bands accompanying Irish Orange walks, no less than a congregation singing hymns in four-part harmony, are a fruit of the Reformation development of Protestant song.

What explains the Protestants' success? Pettegree argues that they built upon a robust culture of communal singing in a way which Roman Catholics of the period largely failed to do. Singing was woven into the fabric of early modern European culture: at work, at home, in the field, while traveling, while gathered at the marketplace or in inns or taverns, really anywhere and everywhere. The genius of the Protestant pioneers of congregational singing was to take this musical practice and make it a part of public worship and religious identity. People were used to singing – they liked to sing – and the early hymnodists used this to enrich people's worship of God and strengthen their allegiance to the Protestant cause.

And of course, the development of congregational singing did not stop at the Reformation:

from Isaac Watts to the Wesley brothers to African American spirituals to the prolific hymnist Fanny Crosby and beyond, Protestant Christianity has always been a faith sung by the people. Nor did it stay within the churches of the Reformation; especially after the Second Vatican Council, the Roman Catholic Church came to widely adopt the use of hymns in worship as well. One might well argue that congregational singing is one of Protestantism's greatest gifts to the church catholic.

But a remarkable transformation has taken place over the last hundred years or so. Many Christian churches retain congregational singing, but the robust culture of popular amateur music-making that undergirded it is no more. At the Reformation, the ubiquitous practice of popular singing and music-making was baptized and brought into the churches; today, in North America at least, churches are one of the last holdouts of a tradition of popular singing and music-making that has largely disappeared from the broader culture. It is not that music has somehow disappeared; given how many of us go through our days with headphones in, it's quite possible that music plays as large a role in our lives as it did in those of our sixteenth-century forebears. But the way we relate to music has changed. We are more likely to be audience members than participants, and more likely to listen to recorded music than live music. We have moved from active music-making with those around us to passive music-consuming indi-vidually. Isolated exceptions remain: parents still sing lullabies to their children; people still sing "Happy Birthday" at parties; the crowd at Fenway Park belts out "Sweet Caroline" at the bottom of the eighth inning. But all the same, it remains the case that there was once a set of communal practices around singing and making music that is now gone.

THIS TRANSFORMATION poses a problem for churches where communal singing has historically been an important part of worship. It is a common complaint in church circles that congregations don't sing like they used to. While some of this complaint might well be chalked up to nostalgia, it surely has some basis in the reality of the broader abandonment of popular music-making. So what should churches do about this? Some have adjusted their own musical practices. If the original Protestant transformation of music in worship was a matter of bringing contemporary practices into church, many evangelical and charismatic churches have done the same thing some four hundred years later. Live music is often retained, but it is performed by a set of professionals on a stage much like at a rock concert. And like at a rock concert, one can sing along but need not; one might also be moved to silent or ecstatic forms of prayer. The music is not *primarily* a matter of communal, amateur song, even though people might very well participate.

There's nothing wrong with this choice to be seeker-friendly, to present the Good News in the context of a familiar cultural experience to make newcomers comfortable. But for those churches that choose to continue to practice the unfamiliar cultural experience of congregational singing, this practice may serve as its own attraction to seekers looking for something more than the wider culture offers. Might this something be joining voice with others in song?

Churches that choose to embrace this mission should do so with the awareness that people may need help acclimating to the practice. To this end, churches might make musical education something not just for children's choirs but for all churchgoers.

Churches might also bring into their space other forms of communal music-making, both inside and outside of worship. Some already do: Sacred Harp music groups often meet in churches, even when the groups themselves are not necessarily religious, and when I was in divinity school I knew a church nearby that held a weekly folk song jam. By holding regular events for singing or making music together, churches can bolster a culture of communal singing. It also provides a genuine service for communities without many chances for casual music, and is the sort of low-stakes event that can make a good evangelism opportunity, to boot!

Martin Luther wrote in 1523 that he penned hymns "so that the Word of God may be among the people in the form of music." Looking back from the distance of five hundred years, it seems clear that he succeeded marvelously. Today, however, this musical reformation stands to be renewed. There is a unique quality to making music together, whether around a campfire or around the piano at home or in church, that other forms of interaction with music don't quite match. Giving up these traditional musical practices wholesale would be a great loss, especially since church is one of the few places where people still make music together in this way. The church will always be weird in a secular culture, in far more ways than our music. In music – as in so many other parts of the church's life – this is a weirdness worth embracing. ⤳

Let Brotherly Love Remain

✦

*In Vienna, Catholics and
Anabaptists gathered to
commemorate the martyrs
of the Radical Reformation
five hundred years ago.*

What will it take to heal the divisions that separate Christians of different denominations? In November 2021, Christoph Cardinal Schönborn, archbishop of Vienna, and Bruderhof pastor Heinrich Arnold welcomed participants to Saint Stephen's Cathedral to commemorate the historical persecution of Anabaptists – a first in the city's history. The event looked forward as well as back: it celebrated the founding of two new Bruderhof communities in Austria, both in former monasteries. These selections from the day's events have been translated as necessary and edited for length and clarity.

The Healing of Memory

Christoph Cardinal Schönborn

WE GATHER IN THIS special place today to "remember the former things," as Dietrich Bonhoeffer famously put it. Here in our country many Christians were persecuted on account of their faith. In this service, remembering the Anabaptist victims of persecution in Austria, we cannot mention each of them by name. On behalf of all of these victims, however, we want to recall two married couples in particular: Elsbeth and Balthasar Hubmaier, and Katharina and Jakob Hutter. Their witness remains important for many Christians in Austria today.

Our Lord Jesus Christ warned his disciples to expect persecution, but how painful it must be for him when such persecution is at the hands of other Christians! On the one hand, then, this service is for expressing our sorrow, for penitential reflection on the fact that such a thing could have happened in our country.

Yet on the other hand, we want to thank God that we can gather in this church today not as persecutors and persecuted but as brothers and sisters, looking upon Christ together, who redeems us from all sin and evil through his suffering. Only God can redeem us from our own sins and from the burden of past sins. The following passage from Psalm 51 provides a fitting introduction to this service of commemoration:

> Hide thy face from my sins,
>   and blot out all mine iniquities.
> Create in me a clean heart, O God;
>   and renew a right spirit within me.
> Cast me not away from thy presence;
>   and take not thy holy spirit from me.
> Restore unto me the joy of thy salvation;
>   and uphold me with thy free spirit.
> Then will I teach transgressors thy ways;
>   and sinners shall be converted unto thee.
> Deliver me from bloodguiltiness, O God,
>   thou God of my salvation:
> and my tongue shall sing aloud of thy
>   righteousness.
> O Lord, open thou my lips;
>   and my mouth shall shew forth thy praise.
> For thou desirest not sacrifice;
>   else would I give it:
>   thou delightest not in burnt offering.

The sacrifices of God are a broken spirit:
  a broken and a contrite heart, O God,
  thou wilt not despise.

Let us pray:

We thank you, dear Father, that we can gather today with joyous hearts, but also with broken and contrite hearts. Forgive us, dear Lord, wherever we have harmed your children in the past, those who are our brothers and sisters. Heal the memories of those Christians who were persecuted here in our country. Forgive and redeem the injustice that has taken place here. Grant that we may now, in this country, bear witness to the unity among Christians who belong to different confessions. For your glory and the building up of your kingdom, Amen.

The Path to Christian Unity

Heinrich Arnold

JESUS SAID, "By this shall all men know that ye are my disciples, if ye have love one to another" (John 13:35).

The threads of God's plan run throughout history, woven together in a fabric that will one day be complete in a perfect tapestry of God's kingdom of love and justice. The colorful threads are lives that burned with love for Jesus and others, the many that stayed faithful through trials and tribulation and laid down their lives in service of others and for their faith. Jesus showed the way with his life, teachings, miracles of healing; with his suffering, blood, death, and resurrection.

The Holy Spirit established the Christian Church at Pentecost, built on the rock of faith

Katharina & Jakob Hutter

Jakob Hutter, a native of the village of Moos in South Tyrol, was a gifted preacher and a zealous missionary. Fleeing persecution in Tyrol, he joined the Anabaptist communities that were forming in Moravia (today's Czechia) in 1529. Despite the great danger, he traveled back to Tyrol several times to continue his missionary work until he was summoned to take on the role of bishop in Moravia. In 1535, he and his wife Katharina were arrested in Klausen, South Tyrol. Three months later in Innsbruck, following severe torture, Jakob Hutter was burned at the stake. Katharina was able to escape from prison in the town of Gufidaun, but some years later she was arrested again and executed by drowning. Jakob Hutter wrote in a letter to the fellowship in Moravia shortly before his arrest:

O you most beloved ones, wake up, wake up for the Lord's sake, for your king is coming in great power and glory! The time is at hand, the hour is well-nigh here, the great and terrible day of the Lord, which will come upon all people, has drawn near. Don your wedding garments, holy and honorable, your garments of love, faith, hope, righteousness, and truth – don Jesus Christ, the Son of God! Love one another with fervor, pure and whole of heart; love as newborn babes, born again of God's word and Spirit! Serve one another in all faithfulness and love, in all things, each with the gift he or she has received from God. Do so willingly and with gladness, without grumbling or dispute! Those who are willing to serve the Lord God wholeheartedly and to be obedient in all things – in them is God well pleased and delights in them as in his own dear child. ✦

Image public domain

rekindled by the Holy Spirit into flames of renewal. These are men and women of faith and courage, building blocks of a growing kingdom.

One such renewal was the early Anabaptist movement five hundred years ago, kindled right here in this land, a calling of renewal back to the true and pure discipleship of Jesus. Through the work of Christ's Spirit, the church had to become visible – a flesh-and-blood reality, a community of human beings who, despite their weaknesses, are a sign of God's coming kingdom of perfect love, peace, and justice. This was costly discipleship – many were persecuted and lost their livelihoods, homes, families, even their lives for staying true to their newfound faith and calling.

This same calling inspired the founding of the Bruderhof community one hundred years ago. It is the reason why the Bruderhof's founder, my great-grandfather Eberhard Arnold, inspired by the first-century Christian church and every movement of renewal to complete discipleship, sought out the descendants of the early Anabaptists, the Hutterites in North America, and in 1930 was ordained as a Hutterite minister. That is why the foundations and church order of the Bruderhof come from our brothers and sisters in the Hutterite church. (By the way, this history is especially important to me personally, because my wife Wilma is a Hutterite and my children and grandchildren have inherited this legacy.)

Fittingly, Vienna's cathedral is dedicated to Christianity's first martyr, Saint Stephen.

in Jesus Christ, embodied and led by Peter and the other disciples and joined by all who were compelled by the call of the Spirit to turn from sin, to repent and be baptized, and live a new life of love in deed and in truth. The message and the flock grew and flourished and spread, in spite of – even fanned on by – persecution.

The church also went through times of weakening and decay through the deceit and cunning of the evil one, and the fallen nature of men. But always there are sparks, embers, fanned and

It seems significant to me that God led us to Austria just in time to celebrate the hundred-year anniversary of our Bruderhof movement. It was only four years ago that several Austrian Catholic brothers and sisters encouraged us to consider starting a Bruderhof community here. In our wildest dreams, we would never have imagined what God would give in the meantime. I thank so many of you joining us today who have encouraged and supported our new beginning here in Austria.

Jesus' final prayer for unity among his disciples in John 17, "That they may all be one, Father, just as you are in me and I am in you," is so vital and important today. Are we all one today? What does Jesus mean by that? How can we be one? What a tragedy that we Christians today are still so divided, not just because we have different traditions and doctrines, or call ourselves Catholics, Orthodox, Protestants, and Anabaptists, but because we don't have enough love for each other. Why is it that after two thousand years we still have not arrived at the unity Jesus prayed for?

Twenty-five years ago, my father Johann Christoph Arnold spoke about this difficult question with Cardinal Joseph Ratzinger, then the prefect of the Congregation for the Doctrine of the Faith. The future Pope Benedict XVI made a profound statement about what true unity involves. It is a statement that the early Anabaptists, I believe, would agree with. He said:

> We cannot bring about unity in the church by diplomatic maneuvers. The result would only be a diplomatic structure based on human principles. *Instead, we must open ourselves more and more to our Lord Jesus Christ.* The unity he brings about is the only true unity. Anything else is a political construction, which is as transitory as all political constructions are.

This is the more difficult way, for in political maneuvers people themselves are active and believe they can achieve something. We must wait on the Lord, that he will give us unity, and of course we must go to meet him by cleansing our hearts. . . . Together let us allow the Lord to cleanse us and let us learn the truth from him, the truth that is love, so that he can work and so that he brings us together. *

We gather today with all of you to remember the Anabaptist forebears who gave everything they had, even their lives, in costly discipleship. Let us also reaffirm our own personal commitment to a life of discipleship that testifies to God's kingdom. Let us also, as Pope Benedict XVI encouraged us, "allow the Lord to cleanse us and let us learn the truth from him, the truth that is love, so that he can work and so that he brings us together."

* Remarks by Joseph Cardinal Ratzinger in a meeting on June 24, 1995, in Rome. Translated from German.

Tragic Siblings: Jesuits and Anabaptists

Eduard Geissler

Dr. Geissler is secretary of the Hutterer Arbeitskreis Tirol und Südtirol (Hutterite Working Committee, Tyrol and South Tyrol).

I WOULD LIKE TO BEGIN by looking at the historical context surrounding the persecution of the Anabaptists, particularly at the tragic role played by the Jesuit order. Cardinal Schönborn and Heinrich Arnold have written the following invitation for today's service:

> We no longer address each other as members of two different sides but simply as

Photograph courtesy of Karl Satzinger

The service began with a dramatic monologue "On the Run" by Gertrud Geissler, showing an Anabaptist fleeing Austria.

brothers and sisters. Despite the weight of history and all our theological differences, we come together as Christians who have found each other and want to learn from one another how we can faithfully serve Jesus Christ today.

Imagine the blessings that would have flowed had this wisdom been heeded five hundred years ago!

Unfortunately, what transpired was very different. In 1550, the Holy Roman Emperor Ferdinand I facilitated the establishment of the first Jesuit college in the empire, here in Vienna. Many more such colleges were to follow and constituted the centers of the Counter-Reformation. Ferdinand appointed the Jesuit provincial superior Petrus Canisius, later canonized, as his court theologian because he recognized – late but neverthe-less – the need for the Roman Catholic Church to be reformed. He saw in the Jesuits, whose order was founded in 1534, a miracle cure for

Protestantism and Anabaptism in his heredi-tary lands, one that would restore these regions to a pure Catholicism.

Beginning in 1527, as territorial prince of Tyrol and later king and emperor, Ferdinand had unleashed wave upon wave of persecution against the Anabaptists, who were held in high esteem by the general population. Adherents of the movement were burned alive, beheaded, or drowned. Their children were wrested from them, their property confiscated, and their houses were burned down, along with those of the people who sheltered them. The Hutterian Chronicle reports twenty-three executions in Vienna alone, with the note, "and many secretly executed," alluding to a high number of unreported deaths. Victims could only escape persecution through renouncing their Anabaptist faith or fleeing. Moravia received many refugees, who were protected by local nobility and went on to form flourishing communities.

Why such brutality? The state saw the foundations of the existing order threatened by the Anabaptists, who refused all forms of violence and would not take part in war, which was of particular interest to the empire during a time of frequent conflict with the Ottomans. The Anabaptists also refused to take oaths. They sought to establish alternative societies after the example of the early Christians, societies not restricted by existing church hierarchies. The main branch of the Anabaptist movement in Austria, the Hutterites, held all their possessions in common, following the Book of Acts. Forming settlements in accordance with these commitments, they also rejected infant baptism. This meant that, from a Roman Catholic point of view, children were "robbed" of a place in heaven if they died before being baptized.

None of these persecutions were particularly successful; the Anabaptist movement grew in spite of them. That changed after the Jesuits arrived, and Bohemia's Protestant nobility lost its influence after the Battle of White Mountain in 1620. Two-thirds of the approximately 30,000 Hutterites converted to Catholicism. The rest fled to western Slovakia and Transylvania in Romania.

Over the following decades, the Jesuits proselytized in Anabaptist areas of the empire and directed heavy polemics toward them, seeking to persuade those imprisoned in torture chambers to renounce their Anabaptist faith. They directed their focus to the centers of Hutterite settlement. The persecution in Moravia started with simple, polemic agitation. After that, the Jesuits began to employ more brutal tactics. Hired muscle was used to forcibly remove community leaders, Anabaptist preaching was banned, and children were taken away from Anabaptist parents. Forced conversions succeeded. Only a very small

Elsbeth & Balthasar Hubmaier

Balthasar Hubmaier came from Friedberg in Bavaria. As a priest and university professor, he initially rejected any reforms and defended the church's traditions. From 1522, however, he started to engage more intensively with the Reformation writings and disputations in Zurich. Beginning in 1525, he advocated for more radical reforms than even Luther or Zwingli, and had to flee to Moravia. There he became one of the most important theologians of the Anabaptist movement. In 1525, Balthasar Hubmaier was burned at the stake in Vienna. Three days later, his wife Elsbeth was drowned in the Danube. This is an excerpt from his 1526 commentary on the Twelve Articles of the Christian Faith:

> O holy God, O mighty God, O undying God! I have confessed my faith with heart and mouth and publicly witnessed before the churches through water baptism. I ask earnestly that you graciously preserve me in this until my end. And even if I am driven from it by human fear or weakness, by tyranny, ordeal, sword, fire, or water, I hereby cry out to you, O merciful Father of mine. Raise me up again by the grace of your Holy Spirit, and do not let me go to my death without this faith. This I ask you from the bottom of my heart, through Jesus Christ, your beloved Son, our Lord and Savior. Father, do not allow me to perish in eternity. Amen. ✦

remnant of around eighty people, including children, was able to flee in the dead of night via Wallachia to the Ukraine. With support from the Mennonites, the Hutterites were able to successfully rebuild. They would later have to migrate again, this time to North America.

The story of Anabaptist persecution at the hands of Jesuits is one of the most tragic chapters in Christian history. Here we find a group of genuine Christians, devoted to Christ – the Jesuits – playing a key role in the harassment and persecution of other, equally genuine and devoted Christians – the Anabaptists. It is clear that both sides shared common concerns but drew different conclusions.

Spiritually, both groups shared roots in late medieval mysticism and the lay movement Devotio Moderna. They both had the same basic conviction that a personal relationship with God or wholeheartedly following Jesus presupposes a commitment made with a mature faith. For the Anabaptists, this meant believers' baptism. For the Jesuits, this meant a prayer of total surrender after completing the spiritual exercises. Suddenly Catholicism had a counterpart to believer's baptism, a factor that probably also contributed to the success of the Counter-Reformation.

Moreover, both groups looked to the model of the early church. The Anabaptists wanted to recover this model, founding churches on the principle of "new wines in new wineskins." The Jesuits wanted to renew the church so that the Catholic Church would be a "genuinely spiritual church with genuinely spiritual Christians." Neither wished to return to the church that existed before the Reformation. Both emphasized putting faith into practice in everyday life, following the directives in scripture as "doers of the word," which presupposes knowledge of the Bible. And both sides invested in education, forming their own high-quality schools.

The suppression of Anabaptists and their hasty expulsion silenced their preaching and example. This silencing tore a spiritual hole in Central Europe that, in my opinion, has not yet been filled – despite the flourishing of free churches, Catholic popular missions, and other awakenings. But, with joy, I can see that this hole is now beginning to fill. The following things have contributed to this:

Working for the healing of memory. In addition to providing historical details, the opening of memorials brings together the heirs of the state and the Catholic Church with those of the victims, the Hutterites.

Such spiritual processes change the spiritual atmosphere of a country, bringing about a new openness to the message of Jesus. The fact that the Bruderhof received such a warm welcome with its recent settlement in Austria is, in my opinion, also related to this. I pray and expect that rich blessings will flow from today's service.

Listening to what Anabaptists have to say today, learning from them, and being challenged by them. The themes relating to the five-hundredth anniversary of the Anabaptist movement can help us do this: living in freedom of religion and conscience, living together, living a life consistent with one's beliefs, living nonviolently, and living in hope.

Let us then cherish the apostolic heritage that all churches have been able to preserve in their different ways for the sake of the body of Christ. There is still much to discover and learn in order to serve Jesus more faithfully. The Anabaptist movement, along with the Orthodox churches (which we should not neglect), can be a great help for us here. We now have the unique opportunity of doing this face-to-face with our Anabaptist brothers and sisters from the Bruderhof in Austria. Let's embrace it!

Of Foremothers and Forefathers

Cari Boller

MY NAME IS CARI BOLLER. I am twenty-three and live in Retz, Austria, at the Bruderhof that was started two years ago in the former Dominican cloister there.

My full name is actually Cari Elizabeth Boller, Elizabeth after my grandmother whom we called "Ankela Lizzie" (*Ankela* is Hutterite dialect for *grandma*). My ankela was born on a Hutterite colony in Canada, where she grew up. Her father was Jacob Maendel. He might have been a descendent of Hans Mändel, who was baptized in South Tyrol in 1537 as a seventeen-year-old. He became a preacher and missionary, and over the next twenty-four years he told thousands of people about Jesus and baptized hundreds as adults. At that time this was a capital offense, and he was burned at the stake in Innsbruck in 1561.

My ankela's mother was Rachel Hofer. It is possible that she was a descendent of Ulrich Hofer, who was living with his family in Steinebrunn in the Weinviertel in the sixteenth century – not far from Retz, where I am living now. But in 1539 his wife (possibly my great, great, fifteen-times-great grandmother) had to watch weeping as her husband was chained with ninety of his brothers in the faith to begin the long march to Trieste. On account of his faith he was condemned to serve as a galley slave on the Austrian military ships. By a miracle of God he escaped and was able to return to his family with almost seventy other condemned Anabaptists.

However, the family was not able to stay in Steinebrunn. They had to flee to Moravia where my ancestor Ulrich died. Last summer I was able to visit the castle ruins at Falkenstein, where Ulrich Hofer and the other Anabaptists were condemned and where there is now an exhibit commemorating their suffering. Two years ago I visited Innsbruck, where there is a monument for Hans Mändel and other Anabaptists in the Hutterite Park.

The witness of our ancestors moved my Ankela Lizzie very much. As a young woman she made a decision to follow Jesus with the same dedication and determination. It was practically predestined that she would marry in a Hutterian colony and spend her entire life there. But God had another plan for her life.

My name is neither Hofer nor Maendel, but Boller – a name that does not enter the Hutterian chronicles. How come?

In the early twentieth century many young Christians in Germany and Switzerland were unhappy with conventional life. They wanted to live a life of radical discipleship. Among them was a young German theologian named

Lizzie Maendel at the Forest River colony, 1953

Photograph courtesy of the Bruderhof Archive

Above: Hannes and Else Boller with their children (Hans-Uli standing), 1931.

Right: Hans-Uli and Lizzie Boller at Forest River, ca. 1956

German-speaking Europe in more than 350 years.

Not long after Arnold returned to Germany from Canada, a young family came from Switzerland who were seriously looking for a life of discipleship. Their name was Boller. They were deeply struck by the witness of church community and decided to leave the Swiss Reformed Church in which he was a pastor and join the Bruderhof. Eberhard Arnold baptized my great-grandparents Hannes and Else Boller and accepted them into the Hutterian Church as a brother and sister. Their son, my grandfather Hans-Uli Boller, was eight years old. That was exactly three months before Adolf Hitler was named Reichskanzler.

The Bruderhof and my grandfather's family had to flee Germany. My grandfather grew up as a refugee in England and Paraguay, immigrating as a young man to the United States.

In the meantime, my ankela grew up in a Hutterite community in Canada. She and her youth group longed for a new spiritual life. In their isolated Canadian communities they missed the missionary zeal of their ancestors. When the Bruderhof founded a community in the United States in 1954, many hoped that through contact with these "new" Hutterites a fresh wind would blow. The marriage of my grandfather Hans-Uli with my ankela Lizzie in October 1956 was the first of many marriages

Eberhard Arnold, who began living in community with a handful of others. At the time, they had no idea that descendants of the Hutterites had survived the great persecutions of the Reformation. They didn't know that there were still Hutterian communities in North America. They learned of them five years later and made contact. After corresponding for several years, Eberhard Arnold made the long journey to Canada. He spent an entire year among the Hutterites, seeking God's will. The Hutterian elders agreed to ordain Eberhard Arnold as a servant of the Word (or pastor) and, at the end of the year, sent him back to Germany as a missionary. He accepted this task obediently. In 1931, he became the first Hutterian missionary, and the small Bruderhof in Germany became the first Hutterian community in between Bruderhof and Hutterite young people, and in this way our different traditions became closely interwoven. I am one of many who have both Bruderhof and Hutterite ancestors.

God is a God of the past, and I thank him for the witness of my ancestors Hans Mändel and Ulrich Hofer (as well as many other Anabaptists) who remained faithful to Jesus and their faith in difficult times. I am glad that today we remember the Anabaptist victims of persecution. For me it is a sign of God's great love that in the twenty-first century I can live in an Anabaptist community in Austria, the first of my family for more than fifteen generations.

God is also a God of the present. After concerning myself with this history, I have to ask myself: How can I live more intensively for Jesus? Am I ready, as my ancestors were, to give up everything – money, family, happiness, perhaps even my life – because I love Jesus so much? It would be difficult for me to do this on my own. We need one another. As a member of the Bruderhof, I am thankful every day that I have brothers and sisters who go this way with me. But the Bruderhof needs you too, and I thank God that Cardinal Schönborn and so many other Christians have welcomed our community with such great love.

And God is also a God of the future. I pray that he might bless this new beginning of the Bruderhof in Austria and that it might become a blessing for many people in this country. I hope that as we leave here today, we are encouraged and determined, as disciples of Jesus, to carry our small lights into the world, that we continue to work toward bringing our small flames together until the whole world burns for Jesus and God's kingdom comes on earth. ✒

Translations from German by Cameron Coombe.

Cardinal Schönborn cuts a hundredth-birthday cake for the Bruderhof.

The Strange Love
of a Strange God

*When my father got cancer,
we prayed desperately. No
answer came. Or did it?*

ESTHER MARIA MAGNIS

IN FRONT OF US, OUR EMPTY PLATES.
"Kids," Dad said. He didn't really look at us; it was just a tentative, passing glance. Probably because he didn't want to catch our eyes and risk dragging us down with him into the opening abyss. It was the day after Christmas. I was fifteen. My little brother Johannes was sitting next to me, on my left. Steffi, my older sister, was on my right.

Esther Maria Magnis is the author of a new Plough *book,* With or Without Me: A Memoir of Losing and Finding *(March 2022). She studied history and comparative religion in Germany and Italy and now lives in southwestern Germany with her husband and children.*

Mom had placed the soup bowl on the table. She was sitting silently next to Dad.

"Kids."

"We need to tell you something very, very . . . We need to tell you . . ." Dad's eyes teared up and his voice broke, and we stared at him, startled. He never cried.

Mom reached for his hand without looking up; she gripped it tightly, with her head down. I stared at the white parting in her black hair. Her voice was soft. "We have to tell you something very sad . . ." Dad interrupted her with sobs, catching himself. I didn't breathe, because it seemed to me that there was a nightmare growing around us, filling the room, coming in from the walls, which were dissolving, and leaving just us and the table, floating in the dark. A dream that could have just as quickly retreated and let the room be a room again – but then Dad went on to say that he had bad news from the doctor. That he would soon have to die. That he had an incurable cancer, and that nothing more could be done for him.

My sister gasped. "What did the doctor say? What is he saying?" She wasn't crying, but her voice was so high, it was as if it were coming from her nose or eyes, or from between her eyes.

"Three weeks to three months," Dad said.

There were no more words at the table, just the sounds of clenched throats.

We sat there, my parents and siblings, like children who couldn't comfort one another. Our empty plates shone white. My body had seized up all at once, like when your foot falls asleep.

He wanted to fight for us, Dad went on. His face was red and wet, his nose running, and his teeth were set. One hand was balled into a fist. "I'm going to fight that fucking cancer," he said, almost spitting out the word "fight." "I

promise you that: I'll fight to stay with you," he added, and he looked at me as if he were crying for forgiveness.

His father had died when he was seventeen, of rheumatism, shortly after the war. Dad knew much better than we children what horror he was fighting for us.

MY PARENTS FLEW OFF TO AMERICA. They sought out specialists. Chemo. Radiation. Something with selenium. The diagnosis – only three months to live – turned out to be wrong. No one knew for sure.

His type of cancer was so rare, there were at most two hundred people with it at that time, worldwide. In the different clinics he visited, he sat upright in bed during the doctors' rounds, his medical files spread over his lap on his white blanket. He studied everything carefully; he knew what was going on better than some of his doctors. As promised, he fought.

He did not take morphine. He wanted to keep his mind clear. For the pain, he listened to Bach's fugues. He'd lie in our sitting room, in front of the fireplace. Now and then he drew his breath in sharply through his teeth. I sat behind the door, where he couldn't see me, guarding him, hoping that the severity of the beat would catch and control the pain.

When Dad banged his fist against the mantel and the music suddenly stopped, I knew Bach had lost, and I would jump up and flee from his approaching footsteps, because he was supposed to be doing "positive thinking," as the doctors called it, and I was afraid of ruining that with my tears.

Off I'd run in my socks, through the kitchen, up the stairs into my bedroom, and into the closet, with coats half stuffed into my mouth, so that no noise would get out. To this day, I don't know how "positive thinking" works when, scientifically speaking, you have no chance of surviving. I only know how to plead with God on my knees, and how to invest everything you have in your belief. Everything. That's what my siblings and I did as we secretly prayed for our father in the attic. "Please perform a miracle. Please don't let Dad die."

Dad asked us one day what sort of secrets we were up to in the attic, and we bashfully explained. He only uttered one word – "You" – and then pulled the three of us into his arms at the same time and kissed us on our heads and wouldn't let us go.

When he embarked on a final big round of therapy in the Black Forest, my brother and I transferred to a boarding school near the clinic, and Mom moved into the hospital with Dad. My sister fought her way through high school alone at home.

In between, Johannes and I met in the halls at our new school. "We have to pray again," I'd sometimes tell him, when bad updates reached us. He'd look at me with his big anxious eyes. Sometimes it seemed as if there was an entire black lake behind them. Then we'd look for an empty classroom and enter into the darkness together with our prayers, just like when we were children and played adventure games. Except that we weren't looking for adventure, and didn't know the darkness, and couldn't make up an enemy. After all, there was no campfire, no imaginary armor, and we didn't have any sticks to hit things with. Just words. His voice, my voice, and around us, desks and chairs. A table lamp gleamed, a bird chirped softly outdoors, a bell tinkled, and everything remained harmless, in the friendly, warm, light-toned wooden ambience of the school's common rooms. All this, while in fact there was a war going on.

SUDDENLY WE BELONGED to the misery of the world. Images of weeping mothers, distraught, panicking children, emaciated refugees – suddenly we had images like these right around us. In the faces of people we loved. In civilized, orderly German rooms, with clean clothes. In Dad – his big teeth set against his emaciated upper lip, above the collar of his polo shirt. In the trembling white knuckles of my mother as she clung to the sink. In the whimpering and threads of spit that result when people keep talking even though they are crying far too hard to really do so.

All of a sudden you know a form of fear that almost prevents you from answering people when they ask you something as normal as, "How are you?" What are you supposed to say?

One weekend, my brother Johannes and I took the train down to the hospital from our boarding school.

There were flowers on the wheeled table next to Dad's bed. His aftershave was sitting next to the disinfectant dispenser. A blood-red sunset filled the window, turning broad cloud stripes black in the ruddy glow. Johannes and I took turns sitting by Dad's bedside with our Latin homework. We held his hand for hours.

> There was no campfire, no imaginary armor, and we didn't have any sticks to hit things with. Just words.

In the evening we went back up to the boarding school. As the train roared on, we spoke less and less. Afterwards we drank schnapps, because that made it easier to joke around with our friends.

In winter they told us Dad was going to die. That our family was now accompanying a dying man. My sister tried to make me understand that when I told her about my vacation plans for Easter break, which naturally included Papa.

"Esther," she said, looking right at me, "Papa is dying!" I wanted to punch her in the face – her mouth and eyes and everything else. But she punched me first, with a sentence that came at me from her throat, past her gums, and between her teeth: "You have to let him go."

To have said "yes" would have been to acquiesce. And I had to either steel myself against that, or else freak out. Because that's the greatest insolence, the ugliest thing you can say about a person: He's dead.

After that, I wanted to threaten anyone who claimed that Dad was dying; I wanted to forbid the world from pretending to know anything about him. How could it know anything? What do we know about any human being? How could someone say, "Esther, you have to let him go"? To where? I'm not going to let someone I love turn into nothing. I'm not going to let someone who belongs to me go to their death.

So I snapped at my sister, "You can't. Dad can't die. Imagine Mom, if Dad were dead. He can't die."

And I began to pray, as I'd once read in the Bible, where it says, "May it be given to you, according to your faith." I thanked God in advance for healing my father. I invested all the faith I could muster. I surrendered my world to him.

> **Your eyes open wide: you've never seen so little. They're searching, but there is nothing. You've staggered into a whiteout.**

Six months later, my father was dead, and when I saw him lying there in the hospital bed, I just about brought the walls down with my screaming. I was so close to going mad, I all but clawed the skin off my face.

After that I fell silent.

The whole world was silent. Dead, silent, and cold, as if snow had fallen. Without God. Without me. And devoid of any stimuli.

I don't know how it is for others who have experienced the death of someone they love, but the sight of my dead father almost robbed me of my sanity at the time. It was like I was blinded by seeing him lying there.

I hear a scream. Mine. And then it was like I was running through a collapsing house. The floor crumbles into nothingness beneath your heels. You have to run faster and faster, breaking the doors down. Not to get out, but to get to the core of the house, to the single, hard, everlasting atom that you might be able to grasp hold of and save yourself with.

You strain every muscle to kick down the next door, and – it's gone. Someone has taken it off its hinges. Or there never was a door. Your feet fly into nothingness, and the back of your neck tingles. Your eyes open wide: you've never seen so little. They're searching, but there is nothing. You've staggered into a whiteout.

AND YET, THIS IS NOT DEATH. Not the final collapse. You'll still be able to hold a coffee cup afterward, though it's no longer worth it. Again, this is not death. We surviving family members – we may still have years in front of us. We still hear ticking clocks and cars driving by. We hear songs playing in the supermarket, just like they did in the old world, before, and we grasp our shopping carts and keep moving, even if in a daze. That daze: we still have to brush our teeth, though as we taste the toothpaste in our mouths, we may wonder what for. Not that this wondering accomplishes much – whether about the objects that fill the house, which suddenly seem so strange, or all the things you do and say. So you go on washing your hair, and your hands basically know how to do it, and you let them do it. True, there are sometimes lapses. You don't really know what to do next, and suddenly you're sitting on the stairs, and you've forgotten why.

At other times, the world no longer makes any noises. There are no more sounds, no more harmonies, no more logical tonal sequences by which you might find your way.

This happens every day, all over the globe, in every country. Again and again, the world collapses for someone without the rest of us hearing it. We only see it: the mute face; the pale, cloying look of a mourner who no longer puts on her makeup properly. The overgrown front garden, the withered plants, and the overturned watering can that lies there abandoned for weeks. That's what people notice and talk about and look at with concern.

I was seventeen when my father died, but I felt like a little memento mori. Needy, but also disfigured in an off-putting way. Shortly after the funeral, when the anger came, I broke with God. It happened in a church at a wedding, as the bride was being led down the aisle by her father. I told God, "You are dead. I don't believe in you anymore." And before long, I really didn't believe in him anymore.

My brother stayed at boarding school; my sister went off to study. I moved back home. We took in my grandmother and cared for her. My mother knew nothing about our financial situation. It was Dad who had run the company. Mom had always been a housewife and a mother to us children. In my memory, she spent the first

year after his death buried under a pile of files, dead tired, asking question after question.

In the fall and winter after his death, she didn't even heat the house, for fear that we'd run out of money and might have to cut other corners. And so it was freezing cold in the big house, and dark. We only left the lights on if someone was still in the room.

AT THE BEGINNING, MOM STILL COOKED for five people by accident, and I remember feeling embarrassed as I looked at the five portions of fish on the dinner table, and noticed she was looking at them too. She'd sit down with a sigh, fold her hands, close her eyes for a moment, but then wouldn't pray after all. Instead, she'd pull Grandma's wheelchair closer to the table, tuck the napkin into her collar, and begin to feed her.

When Grandma wouldn't eat, or began to cough after each sip, or when, because the fork was close to her mouth, she got irritated and tried to shoo it away like a fly, Mom sometimes lost her patience. Then she'd slam down the fork on the plate and groan, "Your turn, Esther. I can't." So I'd silently start de-boning the fish, and mashing the potatoes for Grandma. When I looked at Mom, I'd see she was crying. Then I'd put Grandma's fork down again, walk around the wheelchair, sit down next to Mom, and give her a hug. I'd say "Mom" and hold her for a moment. But then I'd realize that my hug couldn't give her any of that comfort and protection and reassurance that everything would be okay. Only Dad's arms could do that. I had no comfort to offer, nor any protection.

Mom's grief battered us together. Not that she cried very often – but you can tell when someone is struggling or screaming inside. We kids started buying her extravagant gifts. We scraped together our pocket money and bought her opera tickets, and red roses, just like Dad would have.

Women would sometimes say, "You and your mother – you can't keep suppressing your pain. You have to let it out." As far as I was concerned, the people who said things like that didn't know what they were talking about.

> There is no hope without God. I looked for it for four years. It doesn't exist.

First of all, there was no pain. Only death. Death is very severe. It takes away the surfaces to which things normally stick. It's as if every line you try to write on the blackboard doesn't work – the chalk just clacks, as if you're writing on glass. Every stroke – every arc, whether dreamy or precise and concentrated – slips. You're suddenly incapable and stupid.

Before, I hadn't known what a power death has, or what horror it holds – how strongly it contradicts life. After, I'd have to touch my hand to my mouth at times, just to make sure it hadn't fallen asleep. It was hard to get up; it was hard to watch a movie. I basically stopped going out with friends. We no longer had anything in common.

Every now and then I'd try to go to a party. I'd gloss my lips and brush my hair and put on my platform heels and a squirt of the last bottle of perfume Dad had given me – all while knowing that I probably wouldn't get as far as actually leaving the house. Then I'd sit down at Grandma's bedside and stroke her forehead, knowing that all I had to do was put on my coat and go. But that last step out the door . . . There wasn't even a real threshold: just a little crack, between the door and the mat. But

crossing it was too much. Why? Because I couldn't. Mom would say, "I thought you were going out."

"But I can't!" I'd yell. It was as if some unwritten law – *It won't work* – lurked behind every mental decision, even if it was only the impulse to get up in the morning. You become like the ox of futility, biding your time, and grinding and chewing the hours away. With every second, you move closer to nothingness. And if this sounds too hopeless to you – well, there is no hope without God. I looked for it for four years. It doesn't exist.

Back then, I was so pissed off by adults who thought they were too scientific to believe in God, but still quoted *The Little Prince* – those comforting words about a dead person now being a star who looks down on us from above.

And I wasn't helped by the bullshit about how that person "lives on in our hearts," because it's not true. There are memories, but they eventually fade, with no new ones to replace them. At some point you know them all, and some of them make you sick, and even turn your heart into a prison. Welcome to my heart – it's fucking cramped in here! And those old home videos that you watch every evening? You know how the image becomes shaky, just at the point where the deceased is laughing and waving at the camera? I'd think: well, why not dare to say that he's gone for good, and that in a few years no one will remember him anymore – not you, nor me? Because that's what we actually know will happen.

I QUIT GOING TO SCHOOL; I just loitered in the woods. I'd hike up to an old tower above town and sit there, smoking for hours, dissipating into senselessness. My name? I didn't have one anymore.

I remember the sound of the train wafting up to me as it tooted its warning signal at each railroad crossing. I remember getting drunk. Very drunk – several times until I blacked out. Waking up in a park because a dog was sniffing at my legs. Or waking up in bed, with my boots still on.

I had to see a psychologist. Not that it helped. My problem was not only grief. Since turning my back on God, I felt my life was a meaningless coincidence. And since it was already meaningless, why endure suffering? Questions like this cannot be answered by therapy. They can only be suppressed with medications, pushed off, if you're lucky, until you find yourself lying in bed in an old people's home someday, staring at a wall all day long, which is what I was already doing.

I suppose the death of a person you love always presents such questions. About meaning. About hope. As I said, I haven't found hope without God, and I have no missionary intentions in stating that. If anything, it probably sounds needy to say that. But is that so bad? We humans are needy. Helpless. Little. And particularly vulnerable when we love. Because loving never just stops after the person you love is dead. Even if it seems, at a first glance, that your love has lost its object. Even if you sob every morning and seem inconsolable. Love does not die.

There's something strange about that, and not just in a needy way, but in a beautiful way too. In a way that lets you wonder. I don't know if it was up at the tower in the woods, or at my grandmother's bedside, but I suddenly found this love more amazing than cancer. More sovereign, even if it made me go weak. Even if it was love that made me suffer so much. There was something great about it – foreign – unmanipulable.

This strangeness of love began to fascinate me. I was given a new apprehension of God. Of his strangeness. And it changed everything.

Don't worry: this piece is not going to end with, "And then I let go of my evil hatred, stopped smoking, and started going to church every day." It wasn't like that.

But I did turn back to God. And shortly afterward, my younger brother Johannes was diagnosed with cancer. He was only twenty-three. It was a malignant melanoma. Very small, but very nasty. He died of it, ten months later. I can't really say who died, and who he was to me. I might be able to find words for the horror, but not for my brother.

And yet, I can say this: his faith in God was so great that it carried us all with him. He was not afraid. There was a peace in his prayers that I don't understand. Comfort. It was like the love I had and still have for him and for my father. A love that won't let me go, and won't die, and seems as otherworldly as what I've written here. ➤

The German original of this article was published in Speigel Wissen, *March 2014. Translated by Chris Zimmerman.*

Editors' Picks

Walk with Me
A Biography of Fannie Lou Hamer

Kate Clifford Larson
(Oxford University Press)

Fannie Lou Hamer often sang a spiritual that implores: "While I'm on this tedious journey, I want *Jesus* to walk with me." As the title of her biography implies, Hamer's life was a song inviting those seeking equality to join her in direct action for change.

I knew about Hamer's remarkable life fighting racism, sexism, and class subordination, but until I read this book I had never realized the force of her passion for singing. Hamer sang as a child to please her part-time preacher father. When she left school at age twelve, she chanted work songs to keep pace as she picked cotton with her sharecropping family. And throughout her life, she sang praises in church, inspirational spirituals in planning meetings, freedom songs at protest rallies, and sorrow songs in jail cells.

Biographer and historian Kate Clifford Larson chronicles the struggle of those who stayed behind when millions of Black Americans moved north and west during the Great Migration to find work and escape "racial terrorism." The youngest of twenty children, Hamer remained to help her aging father and ailing mother as they eked out a living in the "oppressive and brutal" existence of the Mississippi Delta. Hamer eventually married and she and her husband adopted two daughters, with whom they "cobbled together a living as farmers."

Extensive interviews with family, friends, and fellow activists reveal intimate details of Hamer's extraordinary transformation from Mississippi tenant farmer to grassroots political organizer and speaker of national prominence. A key moment in this transformation was in 1961, when Hamer sought treatment for worsening pelvic pain and was instead sterilized without her consent. This devastating experience sparked a determination to fight back against the racism she had known all her life.

Larson's research digs deep, accessing recently opened FBI records, secret Oval Office tapes, and newspaper archives. She names names – the doctor who sterilized Hamer, the police officers who beat and sexually assaulted her, and scores of politicians, officials, and employers who ruthlessly intimidated Black citizens to suppress voter registration. But we also learn the names of courageous volunteers who risked their jobs, homes, and lives to fight for civil rights. Among these was the activist Robert Moses, a New York teacher and organizer who inspired Hamer to participate in voter registration drives. This led to her playing a vital role in voting rights efforts in Mississippi.

In a searing account of Mississippi life, delivered in August 1964 and aired on national television, Hamer asked, "Is this America . . . [where] our lives [are] threatened daily, because we want to live as decent human beings, in America?" The impact of her question altered the trajectory of Lyndon Johnson's presidency and of US politics, and it still resonates today. In *Walk with Me*, Fannie Lou Hamer's resolute refrain echoes as a guide for activists who continue to toil in the fields for justice and equality.

—*Vivian Gibson, author,* The Last Children of Mill Creek

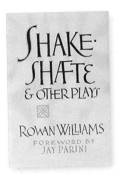

Shakeshafte
And Other Plays

Rowan Williams
(Slant Books)

Some truths are so profound, so dense and heavy with meaning, that the world strains to bear their weight. Tongues still. Words fail. Then things start to get interesting. All three plays in former Archbishop of Canterbury Rowan Williams's new collection *Shakeshafte* examine this point where language breaks and renews: the edge of mystery, a line that, for Williams, runs through culture as much as through religion. One movement unites two worlds: literary bodies conceal liturgical souls. Having devised this theory, Williams puts it into practice in his plays.

The first of the plays, *Shakeshafte,* describes a meeting on the outskirts of historical possibility, between the Jesuit martyr Edmund Campion and a teenage Shakespeare: both Catholic, both persecuted, and both wondering what to do with their lives. Or rather, in Campion's case, his death; the safe house they encounter each other in isn't, as it turns out, safe at all. In a set of close-focus scenes, Williams posits the saint and the playmonger as psychological foster siblings, with twin obsessions and attitudes toward the words of others. A disguised Campion frankly accepts his kinship with the coltish, unsure bard: "You may hear all these other voices," he hisses at Will. "Do you think I don't?" Stalking the ruins of Christendom, Campion curses the coming darkness. But for Williams's Shakespeare – as

for Bertolt Brecht – the only way out is through. To Campion, the multitudinous, mutative babble of common humanity is a distraction. For Shakespeare, it's his vocation.

Vocation also dominates *The Flat Roof of The World*, an account of the Catholic artist-poet David Jones's life and an accounting of the sexual abuse of his one-time fiancée, Petra Gill, by her father, Jones's mentor, Eric. Every character looks for purpose and finds pain. In Jones's PTSD, Petra's resignation, and Eric's violent, self-pitying egomania, we see wounds covered as by "a stone over a well" but not healed. The distance between the truth they seek and the everyday kind they experience is unbearably wide: the characters of *Roof* fall through the gap. That's all, as Jones quips, part of the "Catholic Thing." Mystery encodes, but not discriminately. Behind the masks, rules, theories, and words, you might find God. Or you might just find a mirror, or something worse. One character accuses Catholics of hiding their true selves under endless "patterns of words." What lies beneath these tangles of speech and ritual? God, presumably, but – as so often with Williams – He's not talking.

Except at the very end. In the final, brief entry in the collection, *Lazarus,* the darkness speaks. "I'm what's left," a disembodied voice declares. "You may go away; I won't. The water keeps on coming." So do the words. André Gide worked it out: "Catholics," he said, "don't like the truth." He was right, though perhaps not in the sense he originally intended; it's not because the truth doesn't matter but because it matters too much. Williams's plays explore the fissures of language through which God sometimes appears.

—*Madoc Cairns, London*

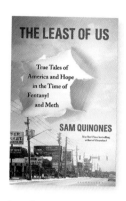

The Least of Us
True Tales of America and Hope in the Time of Fentanyl and Meth

Sam Quinones
(Bloomsbury)

In the 1950s and '60s, Clarksburg, West Virginia, was a bustling city of nearly thirty thousand, a patchwork of French, Belgian, Italian, Austrian, and German neighborhoods with their own shops, schools, and churches clustered around the glassworks that buoyed the city's economy. Clarksburg's proximity to abundant natural gas, coal, and silica deposits made it a natural location for glass manufacturing, and European artisans had flocked to the city known as "Little Chicago" seeking better working conditions and the possibility of unionization and political representation. But by the middle of the 1980s, things were different. Clarksburg couldn't keep up with competition from China and Mexico; its last glass plant shut down in 1987. Neighborhoods emptied, shops shuttered, and the bustling streets became desolate as the population fled elsewhere, falling more than a third by 1990.

As Clarksburg watched residents leave, it saw something else arrive: pain pills, in increasingly large volume. In 1995, OxyContin began flooding into deindustrialized cities such as Clarksburg, following a revolution in pain management that dispensed with "common knowledge" on the addictive qualities of opioids. Purdue Pharma pitched the drug to doctors as a panacea for the kinds of aches and pains regularly experienced by former factory workers. Addiction spread like wildfire, and pharmaceutical companies poured on the pills like gasoline. Heroin soon followed, then the even more destructive fentanyl and methamphetamine. Cities filled with drugs and addicts; the morgues, with bodies.

Clarksburg was just one of hundreds of American towns to be radically transformed by the one-two punch of deindustrialization and opioid addiction. Sam Quinones, in his excellent new book *The Least of Us,* shows how the economic and narcotic devastation of America's heartland – in cities such as Akron, Ohio; Elizabethton, Tennessee; and Muncie, Indiana – connected to other changes occurring at the end of the twentieth century: political turmoil in Mexico and China; the shift of the global drug trade away from poppy and cannabis fields toward laboratories both lawful and clandestine; sugar-filled industrial fast food. It is less a book about meth and fentanyl than an epic about how America transformed from a culture of ingenuity and prosperity to one of passivity and consumption, a withered tree on whose branches the dark fruit of catastrophic drug addiction slowly ripened until it fell.

Quinones is our Virgil through the opioid Inferno, and he tells his story with abundant care and compassion. But he doesn't mince words: addiction is "a brainwashed slavery that deprives the user of free will and turns him toward self-harm in the search for dope"; decriminalization without stemming supply condemns addicts to death; the problem was exacerbated by people acting with the best of intentions. It's an urgent and gripping account. We can hope it will be heeded by those with the power to do something.

—*Joseph M. Keegin, editor at* Athwart *and* The Point

CHURCH BELLS OF ENGLAND

THOMAS NORTH

When in 1888 the clergyman Thomas North wrote a book on church-bell ringing in England, many of the traditions he described were already dying out. Here are three excerpts:

GLEANING BELL

In many parishes in the Midland counties . . . a bell, called the Gleaning-bell, is rung during harvest in the morning, and sometimes also in the evening, giving warning when gleaning may commence, and when it must close for the day. This is done that all – the old and feeble as well as the young and active – may have a fair start. In South Warwickshire this bell – called there the Harvest-bell – is rung at eight o'clock in the morning as a signal for the commencement of gleaning in order "that the children's breakfasts be not neglected."

BELLS FOR THE FUNERAL OF A SPINSTER

At Barwell, Leicestershire, it was customary some years ago, to ring, at the funeral of a spinster, what was called her wedding peal as her dead body was being carried to the church.

THE SEXTON'S BELL

In 1792 a writer on Carnarvonshire said: "Not a century back, before the reading of the Gospel, a sexton used to go round the churchyard, with a bell in his hand, to call in stragglers to attend and hear God's word." Bishop Thirlwall relates another curious custom connected with the church hand-bell in recent times: "As I returned through the churchyard I was greeted very respectfully by a person whose dress seemed to indicate that he was a functionary of the church. I learnt that he was the sexton, but that he also discharges another very useful office, which, as far as I know, is peculiar to Kerry [Montgomeryshire]. It appears that it is by ancient custom a part of his duty to perambulate the church during service time with a bell in his hand. To look carefully into every pew, and whenever he finds anyone dozing to ring the bell. He discharges this duty, it is said, with great vigilance, intrepidity, and impartiality, and consequently with the happiest effect upon the congregation; for, as everybody is certain that if he or she gives way to drowsiness the fact will be forthwith made known through the whole church by a peal which will direct all eyes to the sleeper, the fear of such a visitation is almost always sufficient to keep everyone on the alert." ✎

Source: Thomas North, *English Bells and Bell Lore*, ed. William Beresford (T. Mark, 1888).

Design from the illuminated tenth-century *Benedictional* of Saint Æthelwold

DORI MOODY

The Bones of Memory

Those who care for the dead care for the living.

The burial ground of the Rhön Bruderhof, Sparhof, Germany

ENCOUNTERING BONES above ground was startling. No, it was not the bones themselves, but their vast number that startled me. From the windows I could see them all stacked tidily by type. Tibiae and fibulae. Humeri and femora. The skulls were grouped too, as if to aid comfortable conversation. The building interior was silent and holy. Its exterior, near a church, was busy, full of the sound of my teenage companions as they passed along. But I stood at the window and stared. Europe had many mysteries for me as a touring American high-school student, but this ossuary building, for the time being, crowned them all.

Even today, when the name of that place – was it Marburg? – has slipped quietly out of my memory, I can still see vividly these startling stacks. I wondered then, as I sometimes still do, if God would again call on Ezekiel to prophesy those dry bones into life: tibiae with fibulae; humeri with scapulae; skulls, ultimately, with all the remaining two hundred or so human bones.

As I discovered on that tour, Europe showcases not only ancient churches, but other sites equally holy – town squares where my ancestor "heretics" were bound to stakes and burned as martyrs, cities once home to cousins obliterated by the Third Reich (burned or buried, we

---

Dori Moody is a Bruderhof member and an editor at Plough. *She and her husband and children live at Fox Hill, a Bruderhof community in New York.*

do not know). These places reveal no markers, no reminders, only memories. Their humanity lingers, the very air sanctified.

Even before visiting Europe, I had learned about the finiteness of life. At age fifteen death became personal – the departure of my much loved, candy-creating grandfather. Together we crafted marshmallows until he grew too sick to stir the thick syrup. Then he lay in bed, the sound of his labored breathing filling the whole house. His death brought reality – a wooden coffin with handles for humans to hold; shovels, their handles worn smooth; and earth, handled with care by those who dug the deep grave. It brought tears to the eye too.

My church was a singing congregation, and at the funeral one hymn emerged. It had a pretty title, "Beauty Around Us," but it caused an indefinable feeling of emptiness that did not lift my spirits at all: "Ages are coming, roll on and vanish, children shall follow where fathers passed." The words evoked a slowly turning earth, high-humped grave barrows following one after the other like mountain ranges. The thought of so much humanity lying in the earth frightened me into wondering about purpose and peculiarity. Whether individuals mattered.

High-school literature also brought a good dose of death, as if to make up for childhood years of innocence. In a large graveyard Hamlet walks with Horatio, looking on as gravediggers unearth bones; Hamlet is stunned when a gravedigger hands him a skull, all that remains of a childhood hero, Yorick.

Wordsworth's Lucy, the subject of five short poems, is also dead. There are no loud exclamations of distress or fear – Lucy is beyond earthly existence, safe now, buried:

> No motion has she now, no force;
> She neither hears nor sees;
> Roll'd round in earth's diurnal course,
> With rocks, and stones, and trees.

Lucy's inertia suggests a sort of Romantic peace; Yorick's grin, Gothic disquiet. But I am reconciled to both now.

DEATH, HIDDEN FROM THE CHILD, is often discovered by the teenager and necessarily contemplated by the adult. There was the short, painful moment when the body of my grandfather, sans soul, was in plain sight; and the long, timeless existence suggested by the bones in the ossuary, a matter of memory and reminder. The second, timeless part always overtakes the first grief-filled one. In the shorter run, it is important to remember the living who surround the dead; for the long one, to remember the dead that surround the living.

We come into the world in the flesh; when we depart it our remains abide, and must be dealt with by the living. In most rich societies today, this is largely handled by professionals from the "death care industry." Many families might like to be more involved in caring for their loved ones' remains but cannot because of job pressures, geographic distance, and the lack of a support network. But in many religious traditions, the communal practice of "death care" lives on. The fact that members of my church, the Bruderhof, live together in a committed community enables each of us to take a personal role in death care throughout our lives.

My church calls this "the last service of love." The phrase, mysterious and foreboding in my youth, is not a euphemism, but a simple statement of truth. The "last service of love" the church performs for the deceased and the bereaved is solemn work but reverentially good. There is beauty in the wake, in the simplicity of the wooden coffin, the hand-dug grave, and the placement of the marker that clearly states the name and span of an earthly life. Those who care for the dead care for the living.

This begins with the vigil that starts as soon as someone has died; from that time on, there will always be community members watching with the body. This support is the first step to healing for those who mourn – helping to prepare the body, collaborating on the life story to be read at the service, surrounding the family with support. "Watching" at the wake is more than a physical gesture of solidarity. When the hours of waiting are long, we stand in for family, shouldering their pain and glimpsing their hope.

My father, a carpenter, has designed and crafted dozens of coffins over the last sixty years. Now nearing ninety, he has left notes and drawings for the next generation. The rules: it is a privilege to make a casket; the wooden box design must be simple so the family if desired may assist in construction; it is essential to stock casket-making supplies. No ad-hoc cobbling is allowed here, only a steady-handed touch. These coffins are beautiful and solid, as will be my father's when his day comes.

Burials at the Bruderhof are a congregational responsibility. Graves are dug by hand; after the casket is lowered, attendees participate in filling in the earth, laying flowers, and standing by the family.

From the seventh century, churches have supplied consecrated ground for burials. Likewise, the Bruderhof has its own burial grounds. Each grave is made into a casket-sized garden with flowers in summer, greenery in winter. Gardeners keep the burial grounds watered and trimmed. They are places of beauty, places to visit.

One such hallowed ground is in the English Cotswolds, the unsold remnant of a Bruderhof community established here between 1936 and 1941 by my grandparents' congregation as refugees from Nazi Germany. The burial ground is away from the road, requiring an uphill walk through a field. Visitors trample spoke-lines to the crest of the hill. The elevated ground, the fence enclosure, the latched gate, the momentary pause before entering through the gateway, prepares the visitor to look down. Here are six graves, three babies and three adults, stillborn to ninety-two. Time cannot erase the last service of love performed here. These graves are so old that the human bones under the grass have gone back to earth. The memories of these lives, told to me second- or third-hand, are broken-down too, sketchy. But though I never knew any of them, those who lie here aren't strangers to me.

We come to cemeteries or visit places of death because they remind us of God; they help us make sense of our lives and our moments in time. The God of the universe has a plan, and looking upward to him keeps us grounded. But the slowly bending arc of eternity can also provide such a long perspective that we feel infinitesimal and insignificant. What draws me to lift the latch, open the gate, wander the distance is what lies at my feet. It is the lingering sacred scent of departed souls that gives me perspective; it roots my feet here on earth while helping me sense the presence of these men and women who, according to the Christian teaching of the communion of saints, remain very much alive and connected to us, the living.

In visiting a burial ground, enclosed or open, cared for or neglected, I think of who lies here. I notice the layout, the tombstone sizes, the in-between grassy pathways. The family names, and the grouping of graves. The dates. And where the stones are weathered smooth, with no identification, I look still.

Every life needs living by somebody – how difficult was that living? Here marks what's left at the end of the allotment of days. For lives, whether mediocre or deceitful, imperfect or saintly, were those of images of their Creator, and so can never disappear. ✎

Take Up Your Cross Daily

SAINT RAFAEL ARNÁIZ

SOMEBODY ONCE TOLD ME that the surpassing, supreme rule of my life was deny yourself, take up your cross daily, and follow me.

That "deny yourself" is the work of a soul who wants only to be hidden away, who wants nothing for himself, who longs only for divine love, and who understands that God does not want us to renounce only the world, but to renounce something much more difficult: ourselves. That self-renunciation is a renunciation of something we carry around inside of us, I don't know how to explain it, something that truly hinders us . . . perhaps you'll understand: when you place yourself at the foot of the tabernacle, and look at Jesus, and contemplate his wounds, and cry at his feet, and you realize that in the face of Christ's immense love, you disappear, your tears disappear, your entire soul is overwhelmed and becomes like a tiny speck of sand in the vastness of the sea. . . .

SO, THEN, WHY DO WE LACK virtue at times? Because we aren't simple; because we complicate our desires; because everything we want is made difficult by our weak will, which gets carried away by whatever is pleasing, comfortable, and unnecessary, and often by its passions.

We lack virtue not because it is difficult, but because we don't want it.

We lack patience . . . because we don't want it.

We lack temperance . . . because we don't want it.

We lack chastity . . . for the same reason.

We would be saints if we wanted to be . . . it's much harder to become an engineer than it is to become a saint. If only we had faith!

The interior life . . . the spiritual life, a life of prayer. "My God! That must be difficult!" But it's not at all. Get rid of everything in your heart that's in the way, and you'll find God there. That's it. ⤳

Father Nevin Ford, OFM, *Stations of the Cross #5*, Santa Barbara Mission, California

---

Rafael Arnáiz (1911–38) was born in Burgos, Spain. At twenty-two he joined the Trappist-Cistercian abbey of San Isidro de Dueñas. He suffered from diabetes and experienced the Spanish Civil War, both of which influenced his theology of the cross. He died age twenty-seven. This reading is taken from St. Rafael Arnáiz: The Collected Works, *trans. Catherine Addington (Cistercian Publications, 2022).*

PLOUGH BOOKLIST

New Releases

Breaking Ground: Charting Our Future in a Pandemic Year
Mark Noll, N. T. Wright, Gracy Olmstead, Jennifer Frey, Michael Wear, Danté Stewart, Marilynne Robinson, Christine Emba, Tara Isabella Burton, Phil Christman, Jeffrey Bilbro, L. M. Sacasas, Oliver O'Donovan, and others
Edited by Anne Snyder and Susannah Black

As a pandemic and racial reckoning exposed society's faults, Christian thinkers were laying the groundwork for a better future. In the spring of 2020, *Comment* magazine, along with *Plough* and others, created a publishing project to tap the resources of a Christian humanist tradition to respond collaboratively and imaginatively to these crises. The web commons that resulted – *Breaking Ground* – became a one-of-a-kind space to probe society's assumptions and imagine what a better future might require.

This volume, written in real time during a year that revealed the depths of our society's fissures, provides a wealth of reflections and proposals on what should come after. It is an anthology of different lenses of faith seeking to understand how best we can serve the broader society and renew our civilization.

John Milbank, University of Nottingham: If you despair of the future, the writers represented here offer real prophetic hope.

Hardcover, 468 pages, ~~$35.00~~ **$24.50 with subscriber discount**

With or Without Me: A Memoir of Losing and Finding
Esther Maria Magnis

With or Without Me is an unsparing and eloquent critique of religion. Yet Esther Maria Magnis's frustration is merely the beginning of a tortuous journey toward faith – one punctuated by personal losses retold with bluntness and immediacy. "If God is love," she writes, "then it's a kind of love I do not understand." She dares to believe anyway, although her questioning won't let up. She fiercely dismantles both the clichés she's heard in church and the endless philosophizing of her parents' generation.

Magnis knows believing in God is anything but easy. Because he allows people to suffer. Because he's invisible. And silent. "I think we miss God," she writes. "I would never want to persuade anyone or put myself above atheists. I know there are good reasons not to believe. But sometimes I think most people are just sad that he's not there."

With or Without Me is a book for everyone – believer or unbeliever, Christian or atheist – who refuses to surrender to the idea that there are easy answers to the big questions in life.

Robert Spaemann: I have not known anyone since Nietzsche who shows so shockingly what a catastrophe it is to not believe in God.

Softcover, 201 pages, ~~$17.99~~ **$12.59 with subscriber discount**

Music Meets Literature

Brisbane: A Novel

Eugene Vodolazkin

In this richly layered novel by the winner of Russia's biggest literary prizes, a celebrated guitarist robbed of his talent by Parkinson's disease seeks other paths to immortality.

This personal story of a lifetime quest for meaning will resonate with readers of Dostoyevsky, Tolstoy, Umberto Eco, and Solzhenitsyn. Expanding the literary universe spun in his earlier novels, Vodolazkin explores music and fame, belonging and purpose, time and eternity. At the stunning finale of *Brisbane*, all the carefully knit stitches unravel into a riddle: Whose story is it – the subject's or the writer's? Are art and love really no match for death? Is Brisbane, the city of our dreams, our only hope for the future?

Hardcover, 343 pages, ~~$26.95~~ **$18.87 with subscriber discount**

If My Moon Was Your Sun

Andreas Steinhöfel

Illustrations by Nele Palmtag

Did you hear the story about Max, the boy who kidnapped his grandfather from a nursing home?

A touching story about dementia and the special relationship between grandparents and grandchildren, with full-color illustrations and an audiobook featuring twelve classical pieces for children by Georges Bizet and Sergei Prokofiev.

School Library Journal: With its loving portrayal of aging, caring for the elderly, and the keen nature of kids' sensibilities, this is a must-purchase for all libraries serving children.

Hardcover, 80 pages, ~~$19.00~~ **$13.30 with subscriber discount**

The Heart's Necessities: Life in Poetry

Jane Tyson Clement with Becca Stevens

What are the heart's necessities? It's a question Jane Tyson Clement (1917–2000) asked herself over and over, both in her poetry and in the way she lived. Her observation of the seasons of the soul and of the natural world have made her poems beloved to many readers, most recently singer-songwriter Becca Stevens, who has given Clement's poetry new life – and a new audience – as lyrics in her songs. This book interweaves Clement's poetry with the story of her life, and with commentary by Stevens describing how specific poems speak to her own life, passions, and creative process.

Friends Journal: Clement writes with simplicity and directness, a gentle, probing insistence, and conviction.

Softcover 160 pages, ~~$19.95~~ **$13.97 with subscriber discount**

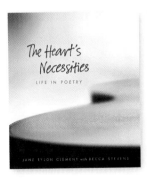

Lent and Easter

Bread and Wine: Readings for Lent and Easter

Dietrich Bonhoeffer, Dorothy Day, Søren Kierkegaard, C. S. Lewis, Philip Yancey, Eberhard Arnold, Fyodor Dostoyevsky, George MacDonald, Henri J. M. Nouwen, Sadhu Sundar Singh, Thomas Merton, N. T. Wright, William Willimon, and others

A time for self-denial, soul-searching, and spiritual preparation, Lent is traditionally observed by daily reading and reflection. This collection will satisfy the growing hunger for meaningful and accessible devotions. Culled from the wealth of twenty centuries, these accessible selections are ecumenical in scope, and represent the best classic and contemporary Christian writers.

Publishers Weekly: Has there ever been a more hard-hitting, beautifully written, theologically inclusive anthology of writings for Lent and Easter?

Hardcover, 430 pages, ~~$24.00~~ **$16.80 with subscriber discount**

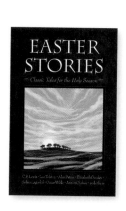

The Crucified Is My Love: Morning and Evening Devotions for the Holy Season of Lent

Johann Ernst von Holst

Handed down for generations, these stirring readings for every day of the Lenten season spring from a pastor's heart. Expanding on the Gospel accounts, they draw the reader into deep contemplation of Christ's suffering, accompanying him in vivid detail on his last journey from Bethany to Golgotha. At every step, from his triumphal entry into Jerusalem and his last supper with his disciples to his betrayal and crucifixion, they reveal the depth of Christ's love for those he came to save – and the hope this holds for each of us and for the world.

Softcover, 329 pages, ~~$18.00~~ **$12.60 with subscriber discount**

Easter Stories: Classic Tales for the Holy Season

C. S. Lewis, Elizabeth Goudge, Leo Tolstoy, Jane Tyson Clement, Alan Paton, Oscar Wilde, Ruth Sawyer, Anton Chekhov, Selma Lagerlöf, Claire Huchet Bishop, and others

Selected for their spiritual value and literary quality, these classic tales capture the spirit of Holy Week and Easter in a way that will captivate readers of all ages. Parents and grandparents will find that children love to hear these stories read aloud, year after year.

National Catholic Register: This thoughtfully curated collection is remarkable for its range and breadth. . . . Keep the book close and pull it out whenever you and your family need a reminder of the great Easter themes of transformation, reconciliation, and the triumph of life over death.

Softcover, 383 pages, ~~$18.00~~ **$12.60 with subscriber discount**

Mercedes Sosa

*The singer who gave voice to her people's struggle
outlived several tyrants.*

SUSANNAH BLACK

Opposite:
Gonzalo Rielo,
Mercedes Sosa,
collage, 2016

Reader, you won't really understand the rest of this story unless you are listening to Mercedes Sosa singing. Pause now to open YouTube and find her 1982 live recording of "Sólo le pido a Dios" ("Only one thing I ask of God") with songwriter León Gieco – perhaps the greatest anthem against apathy ever sung. Do you have the volume set high? Good. Now read on.

IN 1979, IN AN AUDITORIUM full of veterinary students in La Plata, a university town just downriver from Buenos Aires, a woman was singing. Not, she claimed later, political songs – not this time. One was an anthem calling for agrarian reform, "When They Have the Land."

Halfway through the performance, a group of armed military men burst into the auditorium. One walked up on stage and did a body search on Mercedes Sosa, arresting her along with all two hundred audience members.

This was not an uncommon event in Argentina; Sosa wasn't surprised. The military government of Jorge Videla and his successors, over the course of its 1976–1983 rule, "disappeared" or killed outright as many as 30,000 citizens who opposed the regime, usually accusing them of being dangerous communist partisans. A few were; most were not.

Sosa brought the folk music of the Argentine peasantry to a wider audience, and into conversation with other musical currents. She was a singer for the people, a "voice of the voiceless" who used her voice to speak out on behalf of those left behind by globalization, those

dispossessed of the land sold to international agricultural conglomerates, and those maimed and killed by the regime. Her music was the soundtrack to the peasants' struggle for self-determination. Some of her songs were joyful anthems, others angry challenges to the abuses her people suffered.

Mercedes Sosa sang for the people because she was one of them. Her parents were of mixed French, Spanish, and Indigenous Diaguita descent. Her father was a sugarcane cutter in Tucumán province. When she was fifteen, she won a singing contest put on by a local radio station. Her two-month contract launched a six-decade career. Her music was never distant from her politics; her politics were never distant from her people. The title of her first album, released in 1961, was *La Voz de la Zafra* – the *zafra* is the sugarcane harvest.

Sosa and her parents were supporters of the populist Perón government. She took that populism to her music, becoming a key member of the *nueva canción* movement that criticized the military dictatorships across South America in the 1970s as well as the incursion of international firms into local economies. She was a singer, not a songwriter; she brought traditional songs and the compositions of others, such as her fellow singers Victor Jara and Violeta Parra, to a wider audience, in interpretations rich with emotion and depth.

It was not a calling without risk. Jara had been tortured and killed by General Augusto Pinochet's forces in Chile; Argentina promised

(continued on p. 111)

Susannah Black is a Plough *senior editor.*

(continued from p. 112)

to be no safer. Sosa received death threats; she was on the military's blacklist. The junta forbade her to perform. She defied the order, continuing to perform until the night she was arrested in La Plata.

Sosa spent a long night not knowing whether she would end up one of the disappeared. Eighteen hours later, after paying a fine, she was released and again told to stop singing. Instead, she scheduled more concerts; bomb threats canceled them. Prohibited from further performances, she felt that if she could not sing, she could not live. Reluctantly, she accepted exile, to France and then Spain.

She could not stay away for long. She went into a profound depression, and found she could not sing. "It wasn't my throat, or anything physical," she explained. "When you are in exile, you take your suitcase, but there are things that don't fit. There are things in your mind, like colors and smells and childhood attitudes, and there is also the pain and the death you saw. You shouldn't deny those things, because to do so can make you ill." She returned to Argentina in 1982, just a few months before the Falklands crisis brought down the regime.

Her first concert back in the Teatro Opera in Buenos Aires was sold out. She invited many of Argentina's younger singers up to share the stage, the voice of the people inviting in the next generation. From then on, she sang before tens of thousands, and her albums outstripped ticket sales by orders of magnitude. Over the next decades, her fame only grew; many of her recordings were bestsellers. She performed all over the world, from New York City's Lincoln Center to the Vatican's Sistine Chapel. In 2002, she sold out both the Colosseum in Rome and Carnegie Hall in New York; eventually, she was asked to serve as an ambassador for UNICEF.

Sosa resisted the label "protest singer." "It is like an invitation for someone to put a stamp on the songs that says 'prohibited' or

Mercedes Sosa, 1967

'interdicted.' The intelligence of the artist needs to be broader in the face of such possible barriers. Besides, artists are not political leaders. The only power they have is to draw people into the theater." She had that power in abundance – over the course of her career, she worked with performers from Andrea Bocelli and Luciano Pavarotti to Joan Baez, Ray Charles, Sting, and Shakira, in genres ranging from rock to opera to Andean folk music. When she died at seventy-four in 2009, Argentina's president declared three days of national mourning; thousands lined up to pay their respects.

She was politically complicated. At one point she briefly joined the Communist Party, then renounced her membership because she rejected political violence. "All of us," she once said, "whether we are artists or military, must collaborate if we are to keep democracy on its feet and walking." Democracy was, for Sosa, above all a government *for* the people: for the Argentine peasants and workers trying to survive physically and culturally. "I didn't choose to sing for people," she said in an interview just before her death. "Life chose me to sing."

Sosa thought that American protest singers were excessively blunt: too on-the-nose, limiting their poetic appeal to a particular political moment. Her lyrics and music were often softer, poetic: she sang love songs and songs of village life. But she could be blunt herself: "I was killed a thousand times. I disappeared a thousand times, and here I am, risen from the dead. . . . Here I am, out of the ruins the dictatorship left behind. We're still singing." ➵